Alfred Farthing Robbins

**Practical Politics -  Or the Liberalism of Today**

Alfred Farthing Robbins

**Practical Politics -  Or the Liberalism of Today**

ISBN/EAN: 9783337079284

Printed in Europe, USA, Canada, Australia, Japan

Cover: Foto ©Suzi / pixelio.de

More available books at **www.hansebooks.com**

# PRACTICAL POLITICS

OR THE

# LIBERALISM OF TO-DAY

BY

ALFRED F. ROBBINS

AUTHOR OF

*"Five Years of Tory Rule;" "William Edward Forster, the Man and
his Policy;" "The Marquis of Salisbury, a Personal and
Political Sketch,"* &c.

*REPRINTED FROM THE "HALFPENNY WEEKLY"*

London

T. FISHER UNWIN

26 PATERNOSTER SQUARE

1888

TO

## My Father,

WHOSE DEVOTION TO LIBERAL PRINCIPLES

HAS FOR SIXTY YEARS

NEVER WAVERED,

THIS WORK,

THE OUTCOME OF HIS EXCELLENT TEACHING AND

CONSISTENT EXAMPLE,

IS

AFFECTIONATELY DEDICATED.

# PREFACE.

THE Articles here republished are from the columns of the *Halfpenny Weekly*, to the Proprietors of which the Author is indebted for much courtesy and consideration. They were written originally in the form of letters to a friend, but, though they stand substantially as first printed, various alterations have been made consequent upon the necessities of a permanent rather than a serial form. The Author does not profess to have exhaustively discussed every political question which is of practical importance to-day—for that, within the limits assigned, would have been impossible ; but he has attempted to furnish a body of information regarding the principles and aims of present-day Liberalism, not easily accessible elsewhere, which may be useful to those whose ideas upon public affairs are yet unformed, and helpful to the political cause he holds dear.

*May,* 1888.

# CONTENTS.

———————

# PRACTICAL POLITICS.

## I.—WHAT IS THE USE OF A VOTE?

THERE are many persons, who, though possessing the suffrage, often put the question, " What is the use of a vote?" Giving small heed to political affairs, the issue of elections has as little interest for them as the debates in Parliament ; and they imagine that the process of governing the country is mainly a self-acting one, upon which their individual effort could have the least possible effect.

This idea is wrong at the root, and the cause of much mischief in politics. We are governed by majorities, and every vote counts. Even the heaviest polls are sometimes decided by a majority of a single figure. In the history of English elections, many instances could be found wherein a member was returned by the narrowest majority of all—the majority of one ; and when a member so elected has been taunted with its slenderness, he has had a right to reply, as some have replied, in well-known words : "'Tis not so deep as a well, nor so wide as a church door ; but 'tis enough, 'twill serve." And not only in the constituencies, but in Parliament itself, decisions have been arrived at by a solitary vote. The great principle animating the first Reform Bill was thus adopted by the House of Commons ; and the measure shortly afterwards was taken to the country with the advantage thus given it. As, therefore, everything of importance in England is decided first in the constituencies, and then in Parliament, by single votes, it is obvious that in each possessor of the franchise is vested a power which, however apparently small when compared with the enormous number of similar possessors elsewhere, may have a direct bearing in turning an election, the result of which may affect the fate of some important bill.

So far most will doubtless agree without demur ; but, in their indifference to political questions, may think that it is only those interested in them who have any real concern with elections. This is another mistake, for political questions are so intimately bound up with the comfort, the fortune, and even the fate of every citizen of a free country, that, although he may shut his eyes to them, they press upon him at every turn. It would be a very good world if each could do as he liked and none be the worse ; but the world is not so constituted, and it is politics that lessen the consequent friction. For the whole system of government is covered by the term ; and there is not an hour of the day in which one is free from the influence of government.

It is not necessary for one to be conscious of this in order to be certain that it is so. When he is in perfect health he is not conscious that every part of his body is in active exercise, but, if he stumble over a chair, he is made painfully aware of the possession of shins. And so with the actions of government. As long as things work smoothly the majority of people give them little heed, but, if an additional tax be levied, they are immediately interested in politics. And although taxes are not the least unpleasant evidence that there is such a thing as a government, it is far from the most unpleasant that could be afforded. The issues of peace and war lie in the hands of Parliament, although nominally resting with the Executive, for Parliament can speedily end a war by stopping the supplies ; and it is not necessary to show how the progress and result of an armed struggle might affect each one of us. The State has a right to call upon every citizen for help in time of need, and that time of need might come very quickly at the heels of a disastrous campaign. It is easy enough in times of peace to imagine that such a call upon every grown man will never be made ; but it is a possible call, and one to be taken into account when the value of a vote is considered.

Those who are sent to Parliament have thus the power of embarking in enterprises which may diminish one's revenue by increased taxation and imperil his life by enforced service. And in matters of less importance, but of considerable effect upon both pocket and comfort, they wield extensive powers. They can extend or they can lessen our liberties ; they can interfere largely with our social concerns ; their powers are nowhere strictly defined, and are so wide as to be almost illimitable. And for the manner in which they exercise those powers, each man who possesses a vote is in his degree responsible.

There are persons who affect, from the height of a serene indifference, to look down upon all political struggles as the mere diversions of a lower mental order. That kind of being, or any approach to its attitude of mind, should be avoided by all who wish well to the government of the country. To sit on the fence, and rail at the ploughman, because his boots are muddy and his hands unwashed, is at once useless and impertinent ; and to stand outside the political field, and endeavour to hinder those who are doing their best within, deserves the same epithets. When it is said that hypocrites, and humbugs, and self-seekers abound in politics, and that there is no place there for honest men, does not the indictment appear too sweeping ? Has not the same argument been used against religion ; and is it not one of the poorest in the whole armoury of controversy ? If there are hypocrites, and humbugs, and self-seekers in politics —and no candid person would deny it, any more than that there are such in religion, in business, in science, and in art—is it not the more necessary that every honest man should try and root them out ? If every honest man abstained from politics, with what right could he complain that all politicians were rogues ? But no sober person believes that all politicians are rogues, and those superior beings who talk as if they are deserve condemnation for doing nothing to purify the political atmosphere.

Some who would not go so far as those who are thus

condemned, still labour under the idea that politics are more or less a game, to the issue of which they can afford to be indifferent. This, it may be feared, is the notion of many, and it is one to be earnestly combatted. Every man owes the duty to the State to assist, as far as he can, those whom he considers the best and wisest of its would-be governors. There is nobility in the idea that every elector can do something for the national welfare by thoughtfully and straightforwardly exercising the franchise, and aiding the cause he deems best. Young men especially should entertain this feeling, for youth is the time for burning thoughts, and it is not until a man is old that he can afford to smoulder. The future is in the hands of the young of to-day ; and if these are indifferent to the great issues of State, and are prepared to let things drift, a rude awakening awaits them.

The details of political work need not here be entered upon. All that is now wanted is to show that that work is of very real importance to every one ; and that, unless taken in hand by the honest and capable, it will fall to the dishonest and incapable for accomplishment. And as the vote is a right to which every free Englishman is entitled, and a trust each possessor of which should be called upon to exercise, there ought not to remain men on the registers who persistently decline to use it. Absentee landlords have been the curse of Ireland, and they will have to be got rid of. Abstentionist voters might, in easily conceivable circumstances, be the curse of England, and they would have to be got rid of likewise.

The value of a vote may be judged from the fact that it saves the country from a periodical necessity for revolution. Everything in our Constitution that wants altering can be altered at the ballot-box ; and whereas the vote-less man has no direct influence upon those affairs of State which affect him as they affect every other citizen, the possessor of the franchise can make his power directly felt. We are within sight of manhood, it may be of adult, suffrage ; and if the vote were of no value it would be folly—almost criminal folly—to extend its use. Those who deem it folly are of a practically extinct school in English politics. For better or worse, the few are now governed by the many, and the many will never again be governed by the few.

Those who are of the many may be tempted to urge that that very fact lessens the worth of the vote in that every elector has the same value at the polling booth, and that, however intelligent may be the interest he takes in politics, his ignorant neighbour's vote counts the same as his own. But that is to forget what every one who mixes with his fellow-men must soon learn—that the intelligent have a weight of legitimate influence upon their less-informed fellows which is exceedingly great. Our vote counts for no more than that of the man who has sold his suffrage for beer; but our influence may have brought twenty waverers to the poll, while that of our beer-drinking acquaintance has brought none.

A cynic has observed that "politics are a salad, in which office is the oil, opposition the vinegar, and the people the thing to be devoured." But to approach public affairs from that point, and to judge them solely on that principle, is as reasonable as to use green spectacles and complain of the colour of the sky. Politics should be looked at without prejudice, but with the recollection that in them are concerned many of our best and wisest men. If that be done, and the mind kept open for the reception of facts, there is little doubt of the admission that there is a deep reality in politics, and a reality in which every one is concerned.

# II.—IS THERE ANYTHING PRACTICAL IN POLITICS?

ALL will possibly admit that, in conceivable circumstances, a vote may be useful, but many will not be prepared to allow that politics are an important factor in our daily life. War, they would urge, is a remote contingency, and a conscription is, of all unlikely things, the most unlikely ; our liberties have been won, and there is no chance of a despot sitting on the throne ; and, even if taxes are high, what can any one member of Parliament, much less any one elector, do to bring them down? From which questions, and from the answers they think must be made to them, they would draw the conclusion that, whatever might have been the case formerly, there is nothing practical in the politics of to-day.

It would not be hard to show that a conscription is by no means an impossibility ; that our liberties demand constant vigilance ; and that individual effort may greatly affect taxation. But even if the answer desired were given to each question, the points raised, except the last, are admittedly remote from daily life ; and, if politics are to be considered practical, they must concern affairs nearer to us. This they do ; and if they affected only the greater issues of State, they would not be practical in the sense they now are. It is the small troubles, whether public or private, which worry us most. The dust in one's eye may be only a speck, but, measured by misery, it is colossal.

The law touches us upon every side, and the law is the outcome of politics in having been enacted by Parliament. From the smallest things to the greatest, the Legislature interferes.

A man cannot go into a public-house after a certain hour because of one Act of Parliament; he cannot deal with a bank upon specified days because of another. One Act of Parliament orders him, if a householder, to clean his pavement; another prohibits him from building a house above a given height in streets of a certain width. And while the law takes care of one's neighbour by affixing a well-known penalty to murder, it is so regardful of oneself that it absolutely prohibits suicide. We are surrounded, in fact, by a network of regulations provided by Parliament. We are no sooner born than the law insists upon our being registered; we cannot marry without the interference of the same august power; and when we die, those who are left behind must comply with the formalities the law demands.

It may be answered that this does not sound like politics; that there is nothing of Liberal or Tory in all this; but there is. Liberals, for instance, have been mainly identified with the demand for the better regulation of public-houses; it is to the Liberals that we owe a long-called-for reform in the burial laws; and it is due to the Liberals that a change in the marriage regulations, particularly affecting Nonconformists, is on the eve of being adopted. Social questions are not necessarily divorced from party concerns, and the moment Parliament touches them they become political. If one looks down a list of the measures presented to the House of Commons he will see that from the purity of beer to the protection of trade-marks, from the enactment of a close-time for hares to the provision of harbours of refuge, from a declaration of the size of saleable crabs to the disestablishment of a Church—every subject which concerns a man's external affairs, political, social, or religious, is dealt with by Parliament.

Even if only those political matters are regarded which have a distinctly partisan aspect, there is more that is practical in them than would at first be perceived. "What," it may be asked, "is local option, or county councils, or 'three acres and a cow' to me? I have no particular liking for drink; I have not the least ambition to become a combination of guardian and town councillor; and I am in no way interested in agricultural

concerns. When you require me to take an active part in promoting the measures here indicated, how, I want to know, am I
concerned in any one of them?"

The answer is that any and all of them should concern the
questioner a great deal. He imagines he is not directly interested because of the reasons put forward. Is he certain those
reasons cover the whole case? He has "no particular liking
for drink," and, therefore, would not trouble himself to obtain
local option. But has he not been a sufficiently frequent witness
of the crime and misery caused by drink to be persuaded that
it is the duty of every good citizen to do all that in him lies to
lessen the evil effects? And as such good results have flowed
from the stricter regulation of the sale of intoxicating liquors,
ought it not to be his endeavour to place a further power of
regulation in the hands of those most interested—the people
themselves?

Establishing county councils may not touch the individual
citizen so nearly, though it is in that direction that a solution of
the local option problem is being attempted to be found ; and the
supposed questioner has " not the least ambition to become a
combination of guardian and town councillor." Perhaps not ;
other people have, and it is a legitimate ambition that does
them honour. The work performed by town councillors, and
guardians, and members of school boards is excellent service,
not only to the locality but the State. The freedom which
England enjoys to-day is largely owing to the habits of self-
government fostered by local institutions, the origin of which is
as old as our civilization, and the roots of which have sunk
deeply into the soil. And seeing how our towns have thriven
since their government was taken from a privileged few and
given to the whole body of their inhabitants, is there not fair
reason to hope that the county districts will similarly be bene-
fitted by institutions equally representative and equally free ?
And, as the improvement of a part has good effect upon the
whole, even those who may never have a direct connection with
the suggested county councils, will profit by their establishment.

With equal certainty it may be asserted that the condition of
the labourer is of practical importance to every citizen. " I

am in no way interested in agricultural concerns," it·is said ; and if by that is simply meant that the objector does not work upon a farm, has no direct dealings with agricultural produce, and no money invested in land, he, of course, would be right. But even these conditions do not exhaust the possibilities of connection with agriculture, which is the greatest single commercial interest this country possesses ; and, so inter-dependent are the various interests, if the largest of all is not in a satisfactory state the others are bound to suffer.  It is those others in which most of us may be specially concerned, but we are generally concerned in agriculture ; and as the latter cannot be at its best as long as the labourers are in their present condition, is it not obvious that all are interested in every honest endeavour to get that condition improved?  This is not the moment to argue the details of any plan ; but the principle is plain—the condition of the agricultural labourer has passed into the region of practical politics.

There is a school among us, and perhaps a growing one, which, affecting to despise such matters as these, wishes to make the State a huge wage-settling and food-providing machine. If one talks to its members of public affairs, they reply that the only practical politics is to give bread-and-cheese to the working classes.  But fact is wanted instead of theory, demonstration rather than declamation, and, in place of a platitude, a plan. For it is easy to talk of a State, in which there shall be no misery, no poverty, and no crime ; but the practical politician will want to know how this is to be secured ; and while waiting for a plain answer, will decline to be drawn from the questions of the immediate present.

No one need sigh for other political worlds to conquer while even such problems as have just been noted ask for settlement ; and there are further departments of public affairs which demand attention, and which are pressing to the front.  Most would admit that a vote may be useful sometimes.  I say it is useful always.  All would own that the greater matters of law and liberty may fairly be called practical politics.  I add that the lesser matters with which Parliament has to deal, and which affect us daily, are equally worthy the name.  Let one look around and say if " everything is for the best in this best of all possible worlds." If he cannot, he ought to strive for the reform of that which is not for the best. And as long as he has to strive for that reform, so long will there be something practical in politics.

# III.—WHY NOT LET THINGS ALONE?

"WHY can't you let things alone?" is a question which has often been put by those who either care little for politics or who wish to stave off reform. It was the favourite exclamation of a Whig Prime Minister, Lord Melbourne, and it is still used by many worthy persons as if it were really applicable to matters of government. "Things"—that is public affairs—can no more be let alone than one can let himself alone, or his machinery alone, or his business alone. The secret of perpetual motion has not been discovered in the State any more than in science. If one is a workman and leaves things alone, he will be dismissed; if a tradesman or manufacturer, he will become bankrupt; if a property-owner, ruin will equally follow. A man would not leave his face alone because it had been washed yesterday; he would not argue that as a face it was a very good face, and that one thorough cleansing should last it a lifetime. And the Constitution needs as careful looking after as one's business or his body.

A sound Radical of a couple of centuries ago—and though the name Radical had not then been invented, the man Radical was frequently to the fore—put this point in plain words. "All governments and societies of men," said Andrew Marvell, "do, in process of time, gather an irregularity and wear away. And, therefore, the true wisdom of all ages hath been to review at fit periods those errors, defects, or excesses that have crept into the public administration; to brush the dust off the wheels and oil them again, or, if it be found necessary, to choose a set of new ones." And if Marvell be objected to as an authority, one can be given which should satisfy even the staunchest Conservative.

" There was never anything by the wit of man so well devised or so sure established which in the continuance of time hath not been corrupted." That expression of opinion is not taken from any Whig, Liberal, or Radical source, but from the preface to the Book of Common Prayer.

There is an older authority still, and that is the proverb which says " A stitch in time saves nine." One can scarcely read a page of English constitutional history without seeing the advances made in the comfort, prosperity, and liberty of the people by timely reform ; and no man would seriously urge our going back to the old standpoints. Yet every reform, though we may now all agree that it was for the greatest good of the greatest number, was opposed by hosts of people, who talked about " the wisdom of our ancestors," and asked, " Why can't you let things alone ? " It may be said that the grievances under which men labour to-day are nothing like as great as those against which our fathers fought. Happily—and thanks to the enthusiasts of old—that is so ; but if they are grievances, whether small or large, they ought to be removed. There are some who think that a man with a grievance is a man to be pitied—and put on one side. But, even if those so afflicted are apt to prove bores, such complaints as are well founded should be attended to.

It is a fact beyond question that there is no finality in politics, and, to take two examples from the present century—the Reform Act of 1832, which was thought by its authors to be a " final " measure, and at the Act of Union with Ireland, which the first Salisbury Administration described in their Queen's Speech as " a fundamental law "— it will be seen that the dream of finality in each case has been and is being roughly dispelled. What man has done, man can do—and can undo.

The instances mentioned deserve a closer examination, because they so perfectly show the impossibility of standing still in political affairs. If ever there was a measure which statesmen of both parties held to be final, the Reform Act was that one. During the discussions upon it, the word " finality " was more than once used ; Sir Robert Peel two years later declared that he considered it " a final and irrevocable settlement of a great constitutional question;" and in 1837, as in 1832, its author, Lord John Russell, spoke of it as "a final measure." Final it was in the sense that England would never go back to the days of borough-mongering, but there the finality ended. As early as the year after it passed, a Liberal member declared in his place in the House that "he for one had never conceded the monstrous principle that any legislative measure was to be final ; still less had he ever conceded the yet more monstrous principle that the members of that House were entitled by any sort of compromise to barter away the rights and privileges of the people." The views thus plainly laid down have been put in practice by men of both parties ; the ten-pound franchise of 1832 gave place in 1867 to household suffrage for the boroughs, and this in 1884 was extended to the counties. So much for the " finality " of the one great Act of this century to which the word has been applied.

The so-called " fundamental law " of the Union with Ireland is threatened with alteration and amendment in the same fashion as the " final " Reform Act. Already, by the disestablishment of the Irish Church, a large hole has been made in it ; and a larger will be made when Home Rule is gained. There is in England no law of so " fundamental " a nature that it cannot be mended or ended just as the people wish. No generation has power to bind its successors ; and if the Parliament of 1800 was able to make the Legislative Union, the Parliament of to-day is able to unmake it. Upon this point—and it affects not only the general question now being argued, but a particular question yet to be discussed—one of the most distinguished "Liberal Unionists" may be quoted. Mr. Bright, speaking at Liverpool in the summer of 1868. observed— " I have never said that Irishmen are not at liberty to ask for and, if they could accomplish it, to obtain the repeal of the Union. I say that we have no right whatever to insist upon a union between Ireland and Great Britain upon our terms only. . . . I am one of those who admit—as every sensible man must admit—that an Act which the Parliament of the United King-dom has passed, the Parliament of the United Kingdom can repeal. And further, I am willing to admit what every-body in England allows with regard to every foreign country, that any nation, believing it to be its interest, has a right both to ask for and to strive for national independence." If, then, even a "fundamental law" can be got rid of, if occasion demands and the people wish, what hope can the most lukewarm have that things will be let alone?

Politics, in fact, may fairly be called a sort of see-saw: we are constantly going up and down, and can never be still. As long as a public grievance remains unremedied, so long will there be a call for reform; and one may be sure that, though he may come to a ripe old age, he will not live enough years to see every wrong made right. Some may hide behind the question put and answered eighteen centuries ago; may ask, as was then asked, "Who is my neighbour?" and may seek to avoid doing as they would be done by. But, as citizens of a free State, they have no right to shirk their duty to those around them. No man who looks at society with open eyes can doubt that much can be done by the Legislature to better the conditions of daily life. We do wrong if we allow others to suffer when efforts of ours can remove at least some of their pain.

Therefore, things cannot be let alone in politics any more than in daily life; and even if they could, it would not be right to let them. It does not need that one should give all his leisure moments to politics, and all the energies he can spare from business to public life. But it does need that he should pay some heed to that which concerns his fellow-man and the society in which he lives; and all should be politicians in their degree, not for love of place, or power, or excitement, but because politics really mean much to the happiness and welfare of the State.

# IV.—OUGHT ONE TO BE A PARTISAN?

WHEN we come from " first principles " to the more immediate topics of the day, party considerations at once enter in : and to the question, "Ought one to be a partisan?" I answer "Certainly." On the political barometer a man ought distinctly to indicate the side he takes—not stand in the middle and point to "change."

There is a great deal talked of the beauty of non-partisanship, of the necessity for looking at public matters in a clear white light, and of the exceeding glory of those who put country before party. Such of this as is not commonplace is cant, and in politics Johnson's advice to "clear your mind of cant" is especially to be taken. When a public man talks of putting his country before his party, he surely implies that he has been in the habit of putting his party before his country, and that man's record should be carefully scanned. For it will very often be found that those who boast of placing country before party place themselves before either.

"Party is a body of men united for promoting by their joint endeavours the national interest upon some particular in which they are all agreed." That is Burke's definition, and it holds good to-day. Superfine folk speak as if there were something derogatory in the fact of belonging to a party, some lessening of liberty of judgment, some forfeiting of conscience. That need not be. There must be give-and-take among members of the same party, just as there must be among those of the same household, of the same religious connection, and often of the same business concern. The necessity to bear and to forbear is as obvious in politics as in other matters of daily life, which is only saying in a different fashion that in politics, as in everything, a man's angles have to be rubbed off if he is to work in company with anybody else. But he gives up a portion of his opinions only to retain or strengthen those he considers essential. A Churchman is still a Churchman whether he is labelled High, Low, or Broad ; he may believe with Canon Knox-Little, with Bishop Ryle, or with Archdeacon Farrar, and continue a member of the Established Church ; and it is only when conscience compels him to differ from them all upon some essential point of doctrine or practice that he becomes a Protestant Dissenter, a Unitarian, a Roman Catholic, or, it may be, an Atheist.

As with religion, so with politics. A Conservative is still a Conservative, whether he be called a Constitutionalist, a Tory Democrat, a Tory, or, as Mr. William Henry Smith was accustomed to describe himself, an Independent-Liberal-Conservative. He may be of the school of the late Mr. Newdegate, of Lord Salisbury, or of Lord Randolph Churchill, and the party bond is elastic enough to embrace him. And when it is remembered that the name " Liberal " covers all sorts and conditions of friends of progress, from Lord Hartington to Mr. Labouchere, it will be seen that a man must be querulous indeed who cannot find rest for the sole of his foot in one or other of the great parties of the State.

No doubt it is easy to quote opinions from some eminent persons in condemnation of the party system. There is a saying of Dr. Arnold that a Liberal is " one who gets up every morning in the full belief that everything is an open question ; " and with this may be coupled a chance expression of Carlyle, that "an English Whig politician means generally a man of altogether mechanical intellect, looking to Elegance, Excitement, and a certain refined Utility as the Highest ; a man halting between two Opinions, and calling it Tolerance ; " while there may be added the quotation, better known than either, " Conservatism discards Prescription, shrinks from Principle, disavows Progress ; having rejected all respect for Antiquity, it offers no redress for the Present, and makes no preparation for the Future." It was the author of these last words who uttered also the caustic remark, " It seems to me a barren thing, this Conservatism, an unhappy cross-breed ; the mule of politics, that engenders nothing." And that author was Benjamin Disraeli, afterwards Earl of Beaconsfield.

Of course, this merely shows that hard things have been and can be said of all parties, but if they have been as bad as thus represented, is it not strange that England has done so well under their rule ? It may be replied that, whatever has been the case, the fact now is that the old parties are dead, and the idea may be echoed of those who wish to keep the Tories in power, that only " Unionists " and " Separatists " are left ; but, setting aside the circumstance that the Liberals emphatically disclaim the latter title, the facts are against the original assumption.

The history of our Constitution will show that parties bring the best men to the front, groups the worst—the most pushing, pertinacious, and impudent of those among them. And when men talk, as some are talking to-day, of new combinations— combinations of persons rather than of principles—to take the place of the old parties, they should be watched carefully to see whether they do not degenerate, as other men in similar circumstances have done, into mere hungry scramblers for place.

Much of the flabby feeling which pervades some minds in antagonism to partisanship has been nourished by the cry of " measures, not men." " To attack vices in the abstract, without touching persons, may be safe fighting indeed, but it is fighting with shadows." These words of Pope were taken by Junius to enforce his opinion that "' measures and not men ' is the common cant of affected moderation—a base counterfeit language, fabricated by knaves and made current among fools." " What does it avail," he asked, " to expose the absurd con- trivance or pernicious tendency of measures if the man who advises or executes shall be suffered not only to escape with impunity, but even to preserve his power ? " If this opinion be put aside as being only that of a clever but venomous pam- phleteer, an equally strong condemnation of the old cuckoo- cry can be quoted from the greatest philosopher who ever practically dealt with English politics. " It is an advantage," said Burke, "to all narrow wisdom and narrow morals, that their maxims have a plausible air, and, on a cursory view, appear equal to first principles. They are light and portable. They are as current as copper coin, and about as valuable. They serve equally the first capacities and the lowest ; and they are at least as useful to the worst men as the best. Of this stamp is the cant of ' not men, but measures ' ; a sort of charm by which many people get loose from every honourable engagement." And, if we go to the gaiety of Goldsmith from the gravity of Burke, it is significant that the author of " The Good-Natured Man " puts in the mouth of a bragging political liar and cheat the expression, " Measures, not men, have always been my mark."

But, it is sometimes said, the very fact of not being a partisan argues freedom from prejudice. Does it not equally argue freedom from principle? If a man holds a principle strongly, he can hardly avoid being what the unthinking call prejudiced. It is surely better to be fast anchored to a principle, even at the risk of being called prejudiced, than to be swayed hither and thither by every passing breeze, like the "independent" politician—defined by the late Lord Derby as "a politician not to be depended upon"—with the liability of being wrecked by some more than usually stirring gust.

We have only to look at the political history of the past half-century to find that it is the "prejudiced" men who have done good work, and the "independent" politicians who have made shipwreck of their public lives. The former held their principles firmly ; they lost no opportunity of pushing them to the front ; and success attended their efforts. As for the politicians who were too proud, or too unstable, or too quarrelsome to work in harness with their fellows, the shores of our public life have been strewn with their wrecks. The glorious opportunities for good that were missed by Lord Brougham, the wasted career of the once popular Roebuck are matters of history. And in our own day we can point to Earl Grey and Mr. Cowen—and the narrow escape from a similar fate of Mr. Goschen—as striking instances of the fact that no good thing in politics can be done by men who cannot or will not join with a great party to secure the ends for which they strive. The independent politician, in fact, must of necessity appear an incomplete sort of man—always leading up to something and never getting it ; everlastingly striking the quarters, but never quite reaching the finished hour.

It is not only, however, the crotchety man, or the quarrelsome man, or the tactless man, who, because he cannot work with anybody else, poses as "independent." There are also " men of no decided character, without judgment to choose, and without courage to profess any principle whatever—such men can serve no cause for this plain reason, they have no cause at heart." Burke here clearly describes a large section of " armchair politicians," who turn many an election without a distinct idea of what will be the ultimate result of their action. They are of the kind even more forcibly characterized by Dryden a century before—

> Damn'd neuters, in their middle way of steering,
> Are neither fish, nor flesh, nor good red herring ;
> Nor Whigs, nor Tories they ; nor this, nor that ;
> Nor birds, nor beasts ; but just a kind of bat ;
> A twilight animal ; true to neither cause,
> With Tory wings, but Whiggish teeth and claws.

Trimmers of this type live and flourish to-day as they lived and flourished in the age of Dryden and of Burke, and the airs they give themselves of superiority over the ordinary run of politicians deserve all the ridicule men of more practical tendencies can pour upon them. One would fancy that it must sometimes occur even to them that, as in warfare the efforts of two opposing mobs, led by generals who perpetually differed among themselves, would cause more rapine and confusion, and ensure an even less satisfactory result, than those of two armies captained by men accustomed to discipline, and striking blows only where blows could be effective ; so in the constant movement of public affairs a multitude of wrangling counsellors would bring ruin upon the State, where a struggle between two opposing parties, representing distinct principles, would clear a path in which it could safely tread.

No one, therefore, should be frightened out of taking part in politics by the idea that there is anything wrong in being a partisan. A working man joins a trade union, in order that by strengthening his fellows he may strengthen himself; a religious man becomes a member of a Christian church, so as to assist in spreading the truth he cherishes; and any one who dearly holds a political principle ought to attach himself to a party, that he may secure for that principle the success which, if it is worth believing in, is worth striving for.

# V.—WHY NOT HAVE A " NATIONAL " PARTY?

IT is sometimes asked, even by those who would agree gener
ally that partisanship is not unworthy, whether all the old dis
tinctions of Liberal and Conservative, Tory and Radical, are
not out of date, and whether it is not possible to form a
" National" party. The idea of such a formation has been " in
the air " for a long time, and has been put forward with more
frequency since the breach in the Liberal ranks upon the Irish
question. But although politicians as eminent as Mr. Chamberlain and Lord Randolph Churchill have given countenance to
the idea, it has as yet resulted in nothing of practical value.

Mr. Chamberlain has argued that " our old party names have
lost their force and meaning," but, even if they had, the suggested appellation must be held to be a misnomer. It is a con-
tradiction in terms. If the whole nation be agreed upon a certain course, it is not a national " party " which advocates it ; if
it be not agreed, no section, no half-plus-one, has the right to
arrogate to itself the adjective. The last time any faction did
so was at the general election of 1880, when the supporters of
Lord Beaconsfield attempted to claim the title even when they
were being swept out of their seats wholesale by the flowing tide
of national indignation. All honest politicians work for what
they consider the benefit of the nation, and no portion of them
has a title to assume that it alone is righteous.

The inappropriateness of the name, moreover, is not only
general but particular. The proposed combination, according
to the statesman already quoted, is to " exclude only the extreme
sections of the party of reaction on the one hand, and the party

of anarchy on the other." But who is to define how far a re-
actionary may go without being considered " extreme," and who
in the English Parliament is " an anarchist "?

Further, a "national party " must be presumed to represent
the nation—that is the whole of the United Kingdom. But the
projected body, if it opposed Home Rule, would ignore the
wishes of 85 out of the 101 popularly elected representatives of
Ireland ; 44 out of the 70 popularly elected representatives of
Scotland ; and 26 out of the 30 popularly elected representatives
of Wales ; as well as the whole body of the Gladstonian Liberals
in England. At the last general election, 1,423,765 persons in
this kingdom cast their votes on the " Unionist," and 1,341,131
on the Liberal side ; and the latter number could scarcely be
ignored when a "national" party is being formed.

In accordance with the words of the immortal Mr. Taper—
" A sound Conservative Government, I understand ; Tory men
and Whig measures "—the Tories have promised to bring in
Liberal Bills ; but the process will be regarded by many with the
same feelings as those of Mr. Disraeli when he charged Sir
Robert Peel with the petty larceny of Whig ideas, as did Lord
Cranborne (now Lord Salisbury) when he denounced Mr. Disraeli's political legerdemain in perpetrating a similar offence,
and as did another prominent politician when he said, " The
consistency of our public life, the honour of political controversy,
the patriotism of statesmen, which should be set above all party
considerations—these are things which have been profaned,
desecrated, and trampled in the mire by this crowd of hungry
office-seekers who are now doing Radical work in the uniform
of Tory Ministers. . . . I will say frankly that I do not like to
win with such instruments as these. A democratic revolution
is not to be accomplished by aristocratic perverts ; and I believe
that what the people desire will be best carried into effect by
those who can do so conscientiously and honestly, and not by
those who yield their assent from purely personal or party
motives." These words were spoken in 1885 ; and the speaker
was Mr. Chamberlain.

The new party to exist must have organization, and as by its
very constitution all Liberal and Radical associations would

have to be excluded, the Primrose League alone would be ready to hand. But he who pays the piper calls the tune, and what that tune would be can easily be guessed. Liberals and Radicals would necessarily be kept out of the combination, for men who consider themselves entitled to twenty shillings in the pound, and who might be content to accept ten as an instalment, would not take ten as payment in full of some of their bills, and a "first and final dividend" of nothing on others they hold of value. And the Radicals and other Gladstonian Liberals being left out, the remaining party must be overwhelmingly Conservative, and the fighting opinion of a party is that of its majority.

It is thus not an enticing prospect for any thoroughgoing lover of progress. What hope is there of a sound reform of the House of Lords from a party closely wedded to the aristocracy? Of disestablishment in Scotland and Wales, to say nothing of England, from a party relying for much of its power upon the clergy? Of a drastic change in the land or the game laws from a party propped up by landlords and game preservers? Of an improved magistracy from a party deriving great influence from the country squires? Of a popular veto upon licensing from a party to which belong nine-tenths of the publicans? Of a progressive income tax or the more equitable arrangement of the death duties from a party which has become increasingly attractive to the large capitalists? Of, in fact, any great reform whatsoever from a party which places "vested interests" in the forefront to the frequent exclusion of justice?

A party formed in the fashion thus projected would be simply a house of cards, carefully built, as such houses usually are, by those who have nothing better to do—pretty to look at, but turned over by the first breeze. Lobby combinations such as this are hothouse plants; brought into the open they die. In Carlyle's "French Revolution," much ridicule is poured upon the wondrous paper constitutions of the Abbé Siéyes, which somehow would not "march." Within the last few years the Duc de Broglie was famous throughout Europe for the clockwork arrangements he made for France, and the constant failure that awaited them. The "national party" recalls the works of both duke and abbé, and, like them, would resemble nothing so much as a flying machine, constructed upon the most approved principles by really skilled workmen, and scientifically certain to succeed, but having, when tested, only one defect—it will not fly.

# VI.—IS ONE PARTY BETTER THAN THE OTHER?

IT is perfectly natural to be asked, after trying to prove that partisanship is praiseworthy, and that a "national" party is out of the question, whether one party is so much better than the other that it deserves strenuous and continued support. For the purposes of the argument, it is necessary to consider only the two great parties in the State—the Liberal and the Tory. These represent the main tendencies which actuate mankind in public affairs—the go-ahead and the stand-still. Differences in the expression of these tendencies there are bound to be, according as circumstances vary; but, generally speaking, the Tory is the party of those who, being satisfied with things as they are, are content to stand still, while the Liberal is the party of those who, thinking there is ample room for improvement, desire to go ahead.

The recent history of our country is all in favour of the Liberal contention. If two men ride on a horse one must ride behind, and if two parties take opposite views of the same measure one must be wrong. The best testimony to the fact that, as a whole, the Liberal policy pursued by this country for more than half a century has been right, is, therefore, that even when the Tories have been in the majority they have not attempted to reverse it. Every great question that has been agitated for by the Liberals as a body, except Home Rule, which has yet to be settled, has been settled in the way they wished ; and has more than once been carried to the last point of success by the Tories themselves. Not even the staunchest

Conservative would urge a return to the system of rotten boroughs, would repeal the Education Act, re-establish the Irish Church, or renew open voting ; and the Tories who would re-enact the Corn Laws continue few.

Lord Salisbury has contended that, even if the Liberals have always been right and the Tories wrong, it should make no difference to the present-day voter ; and, speaking at Reading in the autumn of 1883, he asked—"Would any of you go to an apothecary's shop because the previous tenant was a very good man at curing rheumatism? You would say, ' It matters little to me whether the former tenant was a skilful man or not ; all that concerns me is the skill of the present tenant of the establishment.'" But supposing, to carry on Lord Salisbury's illustration, this new tenant could say, " I have in my possession a recipe of my predecessor which proved itself an infallible cure for rheumatism ; I prepare it in the same fashion ; it will have the same result." Would one not reply, " I will rather trust the recipe which has always done good, even though in the course of nature it has changed owners, than put myself in the hands of the opposition chemist, who, though exceedingly old and eminently respectable, never effects a cure, but whenever he is called in leaves the patient worse than he finds him?"

And when Lord Salisbury strove to make his point more clear, he did not mend matters much. " It is only the existing party, whether Liberal or Conservative," he said, " that really concerns you ; success, wisdom, and justice do not stick to organizations or buildings—they are the attributes of men. It is by their present acts and their present principles that the two parties must be judged." Even if this be allowed—and, carried to its logical extent, it would justify every piece of " political legerdemain " (the phrase applied by Lord Salisbury himself to Mr. Disraeli's Reform Bill) the Tory party has ever perpetrated, or may ever attempt—Liberals need not shrink from the test. For the Tories, as they have ever done, are now shrinkingly and fearsomely following in the paths the Liberals years ago laid down, with just sufficient deviation to prove that the old Adam of reaction is not dead. Whether it be free trade, or parliamentary reform, or the closure, they initiate nothing ; but when the Liberals have cleared the way, they are eager to adopt all that they have previously denounced, and to claim as their own principles they have throughout professed to abhor. Seeing that the Liberals borrow nothing from the Tories, while the Tories borrow a very great deal from the Liberals, we can judge the two parties, as Lord Salisbury wished, by their present acts and their present principles, and show that the Liberal is the more worthy of popular support.

It is, of course, not to be wondered at that such a desire to ignore the past should be expressed by a politician who, from his maiden speech to his most recent efforts, has denounced Liberal ideas ; who, at various stages of his parliamentary career, has opposed the spread of popular education, the extension of the suffrage, the creation of the ballot, the emancipation of the Jews, the extinction of Church rates, the full admission of Dissenters to the Universities, the abolition of purchase in the army, the repeal of the taxes on knowledge, the throwing open of the Civil Service to the people, the right of Nonconformists to be buried in their parish churchyard, the remission of long-standing and obviously unpayable Irish arrears, and the destruction of the property qualification for members of Parliament ; whose sympathy for his fellows may be gathered from his insinuated comparison of the Irish to Hottentots, and his declaration that it is "just" that the children of those who have contracted marriage with their deceased wife's sister should be bastardized ; whose taste for diplomacy was shown by his direction to a Viceroy to "create" a pretext for forcing a quarrel upon Afghanistan ; whose regard for the strictness of truth was displayed in his denial of the authenticity of a well-remembered secret memorandum ; whose love for liberty was evidenced by the lukewarmness with which he watched the struggles for freedom in Italy and Bulgaria, and the hearty and continuous support he gave to the slave-holding faction in America ; and whose affection for the people may be judged from the fact that, throughout his political life, his name has never been identified with a single piece of constructive legislation for their welfare. "By their fruits shall ye know them " is applicable to politics, therefore, as Lord Salisbury, by so strenuously endeavouring to ignore the maxim, practically admits ; and at the risk of putting aside the canon of criticism adopted by the noble marquis, let me show some of the fruits of modern Liberal policy.

I rise in the morning and go to my breakfast ; my tea, my coffee, my sugar, and my ham are all of easy price because of the reductions, in import duties made by Liberal Governments. I take up my newspaper, and I have it so cheaply because Mr. Gladstone, despite the utmost efforts of the Conservatives, secured the repeal of the paper duty. I go to business, and, as I write my letter or my postcard, I cannot but reflect that a Liberal Ministry in 1840 allowed me to send the one for a penny, and a Liberal Ministry in 1870 to send the other for half that sum. I proceed to dinner, and find that bread, cheese, and much of my dessert are the more available because of Liberal remissions. And as in the evening I visit the theatre, the very opera glasses I hold in my hand are the cheaper because, in one of his Budgets, Mr. Gladstone included these among the hundreds of other articles from which he removed a small but galling tax.

These are some, and only some, of the material benefits resulting from the Liberal policy. What of the political, what of the social, what of the moral benefits ? If I am an Englishman,' I am proud of the fact that no longer is the national flag allowed to float over a slave ; if I am a Scotchman, I rejoice that my country has been freed from the extraordinary system of mis-representation which weighed upon it like a nightmare before 1832 ; if I am an Irishman, I am not forced at the point of the bayonet to pay tithes to an alien Church, to liquidate arrears for rack-rents owing from the time of the famine, or to give an exorbitant rent for the result of my own improvements ; if I am a Churchman, my Church has been strengthened by the repeal of enactments which provoked opposition, while providing no good for the Establishment they professed to serve ; if I am a Nonconformist, I am no longer liable to have my goods seized in support of a Church in which I do not believe, I have the right to be married in my own place of worship, and to be buried by my own minister by the side of my fathers ; if I am a Catholic, I have been liberated from certain restrictions upon my religion, which I resented as an insult and a wrong ; if I am a Jew, I can sit with the peers, in the Commons, or on the judicial bench ; if I belong to the army, and am an officer, my rise is made easy—if I am a private, my rise is made possible, by the abolition of purchase ; if I am either soldier or sailor, I owe it mainly to Liberal exertions that discipline is no longer maintained by the lash ; if I am a merchant seaman, my life is the better protected because of the efforts of a Liberal member of Parliament ; if I am in the Civil Service, I have the greater chance of success because of the destruction of that system of nomination, which, however advantageous to the aristocracy, was fatal to modest merit ; if I am a student, I can go to a University with the certainty that not now shall I be deprived of the reward of my exertions because my conscience prevents me from subscribing the Thirty-nine Articles ; if I am a tradesman, my goods are freed from many a customs duty which formerly restricted their sale ; if I am a farmer, I can vote without fear of my landlord, my lands have been to some extent saved from the depredations of hares and rabbits, and my tenure has been rendered more certain than ever before ; if I am an artisan, the fruits of combination have been secured to me, my employer has been made liable for accidents arising from either his carelessness or his greed, my vote has been obtained, and by the ballot has been protected ; if I am the child of the poorest, a school has been opened for me where a sound education can be procured at a small cost ; in fact, in whatever station I may chance to be placed, I cannot but feel in my every-day life the beneficent influences of the policy advocated by leaders of advanced thought, and adopted by Liberal Ministries during the past fifty years.

If, then, I am asked to justify the Liberal party by showing what it has done, I answer that, by timely reform, it has saved England from the continental curse of frequent revolution ; that, in striving for the greatest happiness of the greatest number, it has in especial elevated and educated the masses, for whom it has provided cheap food for both body and mind ; and that it has struggled, and in the main successfully struggled, to secure civil and religious equality for all. And in the future as in the past, with perfect liberty as its fixed ideal, and with peace, retrenchment, and reform as the methods by which it wishes that ideal to be obtained, it will press onward and upward, and ever onward and upward, until England, now regarded as the mother of free nations, shall be but one of a gigantic brotherhood of freedom, embracing every civilized people that may then inhabit the globe.

# VII.—WHAT ARE LIBERAL PRINCIPLES?

AFTER this recital of Liberal deeds, it may fairly be asked, "What are Liberal principles?" and these it is not easy to define off-hand. There are certain general truths which are the commonplaces of both parties, and no serious attempt has yet been made to lay down a system of principles with which none except Liberals can agree. But there are differences that underlie the action of the two parties which are unmistakable, and are worth finding out.

If one were to ask the first half-dozen Liberals he met for a definition of their principles, varying and perhaps vague replies would be received. For in politics, as in other matters that combine speculation with practical action, it is only the few who speculate, while the many are content to act. And even most of those who tried to answer would be apt to reply that Liberal principles could be summed up in the old party watchword—"Peace, Retrenchment, and Reform," thus confounding Liberal principles with Liberal aims.

That these aims are well worth striving for has long been an accepted doctrine of the party; but, in trying to gain them, we have to adapt them to circumstances, and are not called upon in every single emergency to push them to their logical extent. Logic, after all, is only a pair of spectacles, not eyesight itself : and attempts to arrange human affairs upon too precise a basis frequently end, as France so often has shown, in failure. We long for peace, but not for peace at any price ; we ask for retrenchment, but not an indiscriminate paring down of expenditure for the sake of showing a saving ; and we struggle for reform, but not to cut all the branches off the trees on the chance of improving their appearance.

Before, in fact, we have been able to struggle at all for these or any other points in politics, certain principles have had to be acted upon by generations of progressive thinkers, which have developed and strengthened our liberties. It is, perhaps, presumptuous to attempt to lay down in a few words a basis of Liberal principle, but I would submit that that basis may be found in the contention that

*All men should be equal before the law;*
that, as a consequence,

*All should have freedom of thought, freedom of speech, and freedom of action;*
and that, in order to secure and retain these liberties,

*The people should govern themselves.*

With regard to the first point, I do not contend that all men are, or ever can be, equal. Differences of mental and physical strength, of energy and temperament, and of will to work, there must always be ; and in the struggle for existence, which is likely to grow even keener as the world becomes more filled, the fittest must continue to come to the top, as they have done and deserve to do. A law-made equality would not last a week, but much law-made inequality has lasted for centuries, and it is against this that Liberals as Liberals must protest. We object to all law-made privilege, and we ask that men gifted with equal capacities shall have equal chances. We do not claim any new privilege for the poor, but we demand the abolition of the old privileges, express and un-express, of the rich. Something was done in the latter direction when the system of nomination in most departments of the civil service and that of purchase in the army were got rid of. But as long as in the higher departments of public affairs a man has a place in the legislature merely because he is the son of his father ; as long as in the humbler branches no one unpossessed of a property qualification can sit on certain local boards ; and as long as in daily life the facilities for frequent appeal, devised by lawyers within the House for the benefit of lawyers without, provide a power for wealth that is often used to defeat the ends of justice, so long,

to take these alone out of many instances, shall we lack that
equality of opportunity which we demand not as a favour but
a right.

But if every man is to be equal before the law, he must have
the right to think as his reason directs ; to discuss as freely as
he thinks ; and to act as he pleases, so long as his neighbour is
not injured in the honest discharge of his duties, or the common
weal put in jeopardy. " Give me," said Milton, " the liberty to
know, to utter, and to argue according to conscience, above all
liberties "—for it is certain that with freedom of thought and
discussion all other liberties will follow.  John Mill carried this
principle to the fullest extent when he argued that " if all mankind, minus one, were of one opinion, and only one person were
of the contrary opinion, mankind would be no more justified in
silencing that one person than he, if he had the power, would
be justified in silencing mankind." To all such sweeping
generalizations there are, however, possible exceptions.  No
man would be much inclined to blame Cromwell for suppressing
the pamphlet "Killing no Murder," which directly advocated
his own assassination ; even the strongest lover of free discussion would not be prepared to allow the systematic circula-
tion of exhortations to blow up our public buildings, and
directions as to the best way of doing it ; and instances may
conceivably arise—and an invasion one of them—where absolute
freedom of publication and debate would form a national
danger.  Our liberties, therefore, would be sufficiently protected if we recognized the right of every man to speak and to
act as he pleases, " so long as his neighbour is not injured in
the honest discharge of his duties, or the common weal put in
jeopardy."

In order, however, that men may be able to think, speak, and
do as they deem right, it is necessary that the people shall
rule, and that the majority, when it has made up its mind, shall
have the power to carry out its decree.  Even the Tories of
these days will not dispute this principle, and, therefore,
Liberals cannot claim it as at this moment their own ; and yet,
broadly speaking, the root idea of the Tory party is the aristocratic theory that the few ought to govern the many, while that

of the Liberal party is the democratic, that the many ought to govern the few.

In the days before the mass of the people were a real power in the affairs of the State, this difference was very clearly marked, for the Tories then were under no necessity to conceal their belief that the "common herd" were not to be trusted in political concerns. And it is useful, as showing what the high Tory doctrine on this point really was, to recall the fact that a judge on the bench, less than a century ago, in summing up at a political trial, laid it down as a doctrine not to be questioned that "a government in every country should be just like a corporation ; and in this country it is made up of the landed interest, which alone has a right to be represented. As for rabble, who have nothing but personal property, what hold has the nation of them? What security for the payment of their taxes? They may pack up all their property on their backs, and leave the country in the twinkle of an eye ; but landed property cannot be removed." And another judge at a political trial within the present century went even further in denying to the people not merely the right of interference with public affairs, but even of comment upon them. "It is said," he observed, "that we have a right to discuss the acts of our legislature. This would be a large permission indeed. Is there to be a power in the people to counteract the acts of the Parliament ; and is the libeller to come and make the people dissatisfied with the Government under which he lives? This is not to be permitted to any man,—it is unconstitutional and seditious." We have outgrown such doctrines as these ; and, thanks to the efforts of generations of Liberals who have passed to their rest, the right of the "rabble who have nothing but personal property"—or, for the matter of that, no property at all—to take part in settling the affairs of the State, whether by criticism or active interference, is solidly established.

It may be argued that as the Tories of to-day have accepted democracy, the Liberals have no right to claim the principles here laid down as if they were without exception their own. But this Tory acceptance of democratic ideas is only partial, and a party which mainly depends upon the aristocracy for support can never adopt them with consistency and enthusiasm. The very existence of an hereditary legislature violates the principle that all men should be equal before the law ; the theory upon which a State-established Church rests is equally a violation of the right of every one to think, speak, and act as he chooses ; and the continuous efforts of the Tories to limit the franchise, and to erect barriers against the majority having their will, are utterly opposed to the view that the people should govern, and harmonize with the old idea that the people should be governed.

It must not be imagined that these differences between the parties mean nothing, or that we are beyond all danger of losing the advance we have made. The ease with which we might slip back into despotism is shown by the manner in which the Tories resort to coercion—or, as they prefer to term it, "exceptional legislation "—when a majority of the Irish people has to be cowed. The suspension of the Habeas Corpus Act, the abolition of trial by jury, the extinction of liberty of the press, and the denial of the right of public meeting have been frequently enacted against the majority of the people of Ireland, because their views on the political situation have not accorded with those of the majority of the people of England. And though they have all failed, and repeatedly failed, a variation of the same old plan is put in operation to-day as if it were a newly-discovered and infallible remedy for every popular ill.

Easy-going folk are apt to reply that, as these things concern only Ireland, it is of no special moment to ourselves, and that England is safe from any revival of a despotic system. Even if this were true it would be false morality, and false morality makes bad politics. But it is not true. Despotism is a disease which spreads, and any development of it applied to one part of the body politic might, in conceivable circumstances, be used as a precedent to apply it to the whole. And if it be said that in these happy days the men of England have the undisputed right to think as they like and talk as they will, it can be answered that not one of the shackles upon freedom of thought and freedom of action has been voluntarily struck off by the Tories, and that it is only lately that they prevented a member of Parliament for years from taking the seat to which he had been four times elected, because he avowed what he believed upon theological questions.

The difference between the two parties, even in the present general acceptance of a democratic system, may be put in words once used by Mr. Chamberlain—"It is the essential condition, the cardinal principle of Liberalism, that we should recognize rights, and not merely confer favours." With us, the suffrage is the right of every free citizen ; with the Tories, it is a favour conferred upon the working by the moneyed classes. We demand religious equality ; the Tories are willing to give toleration. But favours we do not ask, and toleration we will not have.

Liberals, in fact, are prepared substantially to subscribe to the principles laid down more than a century since in the American Declaration of Independence—a document which sounded the knell of despotism on its own side of the Atlantic, and awoke echoes which shook down another despotism on ours. "We hold," said that document, "these truths to be self-evident—that all men are created equal ; that they are endowed by their Creator with certain unalienable rights ; that among these are life, liberty, and the pursuit of happiness. That to secure these rights, governments are instituted among men, deriving their just powers from the consent of the governed ; that whenever any form of government becomes destructive of these ends, it is the right of the people to alter or to abolish it, and to institute a new government, laying its foundation on such principles and organizing its powers in such form as to them shall seem most likely to effect their safety and happiness."

These, broadly speaking, are Liberal principles ; and when one has absorbed them thoroughly, there comes to him that Liberal sentiment, that enthusiasm for his fellows, which feels a blow struck at any man's freedom, in any part of the whole world, as keenly as if it were struck at his own.

# VIII.—ARE LIBERALS AND RADICALS AGREED?

IT may be thought that by dealing only with "the fundamental principles of the Liberal party," the Radicals were put aside as if they had no separate existence; and to a large extent this is true, for Radicals are simply advanced Liberals. The principles just asserted are common to all members of the progressive party. There are differences as to the time at which certain measures directly flowing from them shall become a portion of the party's platform; and that is all.

A great deal of the prejudice which used to exist against those called "Radicals" has died away, but traces of it linger still; and it will be well to see what Radicalism, as a phase of Liberalism, really is. It may sound strange to be told that the Whigs were the Radicals of an earlier day, and that they sometimes carried their Radicalism to the point of revolution. In these times it is becoming increasingly doubtful whether those who call themselves by what was once the honourable title of "Whig" have any claim to be considered members of the Liberal party; and there are many who consider that they are now more truly conservative than the Conservatives themselves. The Whigs tell us that they are only acting as the drag on the wheel; but this implies that we are always going down hill. That we do not believe. We hold that we are progressing; and a drag which would act upon the coach as it climbs the hill is a product neither of prudence nor common sense.

The bulk of the party of progress in these days may be said to combine Liberal traditions with Radical instincts. The two can mingle with the utmost ease, and, though they may run side by side for some time before they join, the steady stream of the one and the rapid rush of the other always unite at last in one broad river of liberalizing sentiment, which fertilizes as it flows.

From the time when Bolingbroke wrote of some measure that "such a remedy might have wrought a *radical cure* of the evil that threatens our constitution" to the date, a century later, when those who wished to introduce a "radical reform" into our representative system were called by the name, there were many Whigs who talked Radicalism without being aware of it; but when the title had been given to a section of the Liberal party, it became for a long period a term of reproach. Mr. Gladstone, once speaking at Birmingham, quoted a definition of the early Radicals which described them as men "whose temper had been soured against the laws and institutions of their country;" and he admitted that there was much justification for their having been so. But one can quite understand that men of a soured temper were not likely to be popular with the placid politician who stayed at home, or the place-hunter who went to the House of Commons; and the bad meaning, once attached to the name, remained affixed to it for a very long time.

Mr. Gladstone, in the speech referred to, was the first great English statesman to try and remove the reproach; and this he did by defining a Radical as "a man who is in earnest." This was flattering, but as a definition lacked precision, for Tories are often in desperate earnest. Many Radicals would assert that the very name—coming, as it of course does, from the Latin word for "root"—tells everything; that it signifies that they go to the root of all matters with which they deal, and that, where reform is needed, it is a root and branch reform they advocate.

To this it may be replied that to go to the root of everything is not always practicable and is not necessarily judicious. If a tree be thoroughly rotten, if it be liable to be shaken to the ground by the first blast, and thereby to injure all its surroundings, it should certainly be cut down, and as soon as it conveniently can be. But if the tree has only two or three rotten branches, there is no necessity to go to its root. If one does, it will very probably kill a good tree which, with only the decayed portions removed, might bear valuable fruit. As with trees, so with institutions ; and what seems to be forgotten by many who call themselves Radical is that, in a highly-complex civilization such as ours, we have to bear with some things that are far from ideal, simply because of that force of do-nothingness which, powerful in mechanics, is as great in political life.

A friend who has long worked in the Liberal cause once observed : " The misfortune is that it is difficult to tell what a man's ideas of public policy are from the mere fact of his calling himself a Radical. If by Radical is meant Advanced Liberal— a Liberal determined to push forward with all practicable speed, a Liberal who is in earnest—then I can understand it, and I will readily take the name. But if by Radical is meant a somewhat hysterical creature, who is ready to fight for every fad that tickles his fancy, as he seems to be in some cases, or a cantankerous being whose crotchets compel him to sever himself from all other workers, as he is in others ; if he is of the extreme Spencerian school, and demurs to most legislation on the ground that it is over-legislation, or of the extreme Socialist school, and demands that Government shall do everything, and individual effort be practically strangled by force of law, I am not a Radical, and hope never to be called one."

But the practical Radicalism which is one of the greatest factors in Liberal policy at the present day, is far removed from the schools just depicted. The reasonable Radical is not a believer in any of the schemes—as old as the hills and yet unblushingly preached to-day—which, by some legislative hocus-pocus, some supreme stroke of statecraft, will " put a pot on every fire and a fowl in every pot ; " will endow each widow and give a portion to all unmarried girls ; will feed the poor without burdening the community ; and will make all the crooked paths straight without undue trouble to ourselves. He holds that

> Diseases desperate grown
> By desperate remedies are removed,
> Or not at all ;

4

but he does not consider all diseases to be of the character described; he does not refuse the half-loaf because for the moment the whole one is impossible of attainment; and he does not repudiate other honest workers in the cause of progress because their pace is not quite so swift, and their point of view somewhat different.

In the constant striving after a high ideal, there is in the Radical's heart a resolute desire to emerge from any rut into which politics may have degenerated. For the very reason of his existence is that, if there be an abuse in Church or State which agitation and argument can remove, all honest endeavours must be made to remove it. He cannot forget that many abuses have been got rid of by these means, and he profits by the lesson to attack those which remain. It is their extinction at which he aims. Earnestness, enthusiasm, and devotion to principle are his weapons, and these he will not waste in fruitless longings after a perfect State, but will use them to make the State we possess as perfect as is possible. In all things he will aim at the practical; he will remember that compromise is not necessarily cowardly, and that it is possible for those who disagree with him to be as honest in their views and as pure in their aims as himself. And in striving for the greatest happiness of the greatest number, he will never forget that the greatest number is all.

The answer may be made that this is an ideal Radical, and that the real article is very different. So many have been taught to think, but they are wrong. There are some rough diamonds in the Radical party, it is true; but, so long as they be diamonds, we can afford to wait a little for the polish. They are bigoted it may be said, and bigotry is hateful. But bigots are just as useful to a reform as backwoodsmen to a new community; they clear away obstacles from which gentler men would shrink; rough and occasionally awkward to deal with, they make the pathways along which others can move.

But, it is sometimes asked, where are the old philosophical Radicals—men of the stamp of Bentham, and Grote, and James Mill? Dead, all of them, having done their life's work faithfully and well; and their successors have to look at politics from the standpoint of to-day, and not of half a century ago. And when the Tories say that these were especially admirable men, it must not be forgotten that their ideas were as strongly opposed and their persons as bitterly assailed by the Tories of their own day as are the ideas and the persons of the unphilosophical Radicals—if they are to be called so—of this present year of grace.

The Radicals of to-day have their faults, and there shall be no attempt to conceal them. Many who call themselves by the name discredit it by impatience of opposition, readiness to attribute interested motives to those differing from them, and intolerance towards those who exercise in another direction what they emphatically claim for themselves—absolute freedom of thought, speech, and action. Some among them also are prone to be led aside by a catching phrase, without troubling to ask what it really means ; and, in order to strengthen their forces, allow themselves to be connected with any movement that may for the moment be popular. And even more, but these of a much higher stamp, are carried away by the dangerous delusion that in any political system can be found perfect happiness.

No honest Radical will deny the existence of these faults or be offended that they should be pointed out. But the essential purity of aim and depth of honest fervour possessed by the Radicals of this country deserves all recognition. At heavy sacrifice to themselves they have led the van in every great political movement, and their instinct has been proved to be right. They have held aloft the lamp of liberty in times of depression when Liberals of feebler soul would have hidden it beneath a bushel in the hope of brighter days. And, even were their failings more far-reaching than any that can be urged against them, their services as pioneers of freedom would entitle them to the heartiest thanks of all who have entered into their heritage because of the efforts the Radicals have made.

Radicals and Liberals, then, are agreed as to principle though they differ in methods, for the Liberal is a very good lantern, but a lantern which requires lighting ; and it is the Radical who strikes the match.

# IX.—WHAT ARE THE LIBERALS DOING?

THERE has now been told a great deal about the principles which the Liberals entertain, and a list has been given of the many glorious things the Liberals have done ; but the question of greatest immediate interest is what the Liberals are doing, for we cannot live upon the exploits of the past, but upon the performances of the present and the promises of the future.

Although the Liberals at this moment are concentrating their main attention upon the question of self-government for Ireland, there are other important matters affecting the remainder of the United Kingdom which occupy a place in their thoughts, and which will form their future party " cry."

It has, of course, often been remarked that men when in Opposition call out for a great deal which they fail to accomplish when in office ; but discredit does not of necessity ensue. It certainly shows that in certain instances men do not come up to their ideal, but does that prove the ideal to be wrong? Does it not rather prove that those who adopted it, like mortal men everywhere and in all ages, were fallible ? Despite every drawback and every backsliding—and such drawbacks and backslidings are admittedly many—it is better to have a high ideal and fail frequently to attain it, than to have no definiteness of purpose and take the chance of blundering into the right.

None should think lightly of the power of a popular cry. It was with the shout of the leading tenet of their new creed that the Arabs fought their way from Mecca to Madrid ; it was with the exclamation " Jerusalem is lost !" that the Crusaders marched across Europe to battle with the Saracen ; it was with the

device " For God and the Protestant Religion " that William of
Orange swept the Stuarts out of Britain ; and it was with the
burning words of the " Marseillaise " that the raw levies of
France defied and defeated the trained armies of Europe. For
the popular cry voices the popular emotion, and when the
popular emotion is at its height its force is irresistible.

To touch the heart of the people must, therefore, be one aim
of any democratic party ; and that is why the politician who
makes no allowance for human passion, prejudice, or pre-
possession is a mere dreamer, who deserves and is bound to
fail. The fashion of the German philosopher who, on being
asked to describe a camel, evolved the animal from his inner
consciousness, is that in which some of our political guides
create their ideas of the world around them. They sit in the
same armchair as of old, and do not perceive how the conditions
have changed. They continue to imagine that the clique of
some club-house controls public events, and that the whisper of
the party whip is all-powerful with the constituencies. They
do not recognize that voters are not now an appanage of the
Reform or the Carlton, because the groove they have hollowed
out for themselves is too deep to allow them to look over the
edge. But in nothing more than in politics is it true that the
proper study of mankind is man.

And, if one moves among the masses of his fellows, he will
find a growing desire to put to practical use the tools the State
has given them. Household suffrage and the ballot were not an
end but a means, and the question which politicians should ask
themselves in this day of comparative quiet is to what end these
means shall be put. Those who talk with working men know
that there is a vague discontent with things as they are, which,
if not directed into proper channels, may become dangerous, for
in many quarters the old ignorant impatience of taxation is
giving place to an ignorant impatience of the rich. No good
will come of shutting our eyes to the existence of this feeling ;
the question is how in the fairest and fittest manner it can be
eradicated.

It must not be forgotten that the working classes have only
recently obtained direct political power, and that there is still

much uncertainty among them as to the best uses to which it can be put. There would be nothing immoral in their using that power to better their own interests. Men, after all, are but mortal ; and, just as the upper classes before 1832 used the power of Parliament to further their own ends, and just as later the middle classes, when they were uppermost, attended carefully to themselves, so the working classes will do when they recognize their strength. And this is only saying that men being as they are, " Number One " will be the most prominent figure in their political calculations, whether that number represents a peer of the realm or a labourer on the roads.

This is not the place to enter into the question of how far the State ought to interfere with social problems. The fact to be emphasized is that there is an increasing body of opinion, especially among the working classes, that certain social problems will have to be attended to. Any politician who attempts to forecast the future—more especially any Liberal who wishes to draw up a party programme—must recognize this, and act according to his convictions after fully considering it.

The politics of the future will, therefore, have a distinctly social tinge, but they must include also many questions which are regarded to-day, and will continue to be regarded, as of a partisan character. It is requisite, then, to the right understanding of Liberal policy that a broad view should be taken of the matters which are likely within no distant date to become planks of the party platform. Calm discussion now may save misapprehension then, and if we can see exactly whither we are going, we shall be able with the more certainty to pursue our journey. And if, in the course of the discussion, what at the first blush appears an extreme view is taken, remember always the old truth that half a loaf is better than no bread—that is, if the half-loaf be good bread and honestly earned, and not to be accepted as an equivalent for the whole, if that be wished for and attainable.

Subject to this condition, the Liberal party can do no better than consider what is likely to come within the scope of its future exertions ; and although it is right to take up one thing at a time in order that that one thing may be done well, good will be effected by at once endeavouring to answer the main questions now before us. Upon the spirit in which these are discussed, and the manner in which they are replied to, much of the future of popular government in England will depend. The scientific naturalist of to-day tells us that it is an idle fable which states that the ostrich hides its head in the sand with the idea of escaping observation ; but really so many of our leading politicians execute a variation of this manœuvre in regard to the questions of the future, that the ostrich need not be ashamed to be stupid in such eminent company.

A preliminary to the discussion in detail of questions which go to the root of many of the most important matters in politics is a resolution not to be led aside from any course one may think right by the fear of being called hard names, or by the use of certain venerable but weather-worn phrases. It is so easy to endeavour to damage political opponents by applying to them such names as Separatists or Socialists, Atheists or Revolutionaries, that one cannot wonder that the practice is frequently adopted by the Tory party. But hard words break no bones, and the politician who is frightened by a nickname may be a very estimable person, but he is no good in a fight.

Similarly we can afford to despise certain of the phrases which with some politicians do duty for argument. No one should be turned back from doing what he thought to be right in the circumstances of to-day by being reminded of that mysterious entity " the wisdom of our ancestors." What sane man would conduct a shop as it was conducted 500 years since ? And where would science be if we still swore by the skill of the alchemists? Accumulated experience in the varied transactions of life is held to improve man's judgment and capacity ; why should it not be similarly held to improve the judgment and capacity of States? Let any one who sighs after the wisdom of our ancestors apply in imagination the political maxims in vogue even a hundred years ago to the affairs of this present, and then let him say honestly whether he would wish by them to be governed.

Another fine-crusted example of a worn-out phrase is that in praise of " the good old times." We are invited to believe that, in some unnamed age, England was better and brighter, and her people happier and richer, than to-day, and mainly because rulers were obeyed in all things and no questions asked. But particulars are lacking ; and these sketches of the glories of "the good old times" are like nothing so much as Chinese pictures, displaying an abundance of colour but no perspective, an amazing imagination but an absence of exact likeness to anything ever seen by mortal man.

"Dangerous innovations" also is a phrase at which no one should be alarmed. No great good has ever been accomplished without many excellent persons considering it a "dangerous innovation." The Scribes and the Pharisees, and, after them, the Roman Empire, denounced and persecuted the Christian religion upon this ground ; the most powerful Church in Christendom, with similar belief and similar lack of success, used every engine at its command to suppress the Reformation As in religious so in political affairs. King John would doubtless have described Magna Charta in just such terms ; the partisans of Charles the First certainly held that opinion concerning the demand of Parliament to control the Church, the army, and the monarchy itself; the opponents of every measure of reform—political, social, or religious—have used the phrase. From the greatest to the smallest reform it has been the same. In the early years of this century a Parochial Schools Bill, because it did not give all power to the clergy, was opposed by the then Archbishop of Canterbury with the words, "Their lordships' prudence would, and must, guard against innovations that might shake the foundations of religion." When, in later times, gas was introduced, the aristocratic dwellers in western London protested with equal force against such an innovation as the new illuminant ; and Lord Beaconsfield, in the opening chapters of the last of his novels, sketched with ironic pen the attempts of high-born ladies to prevent the spread of light. Thus, in things sublime and in things ridiculous, the cry of "dangerous innovation" has been raised until it has been rendered contemptible.

Equally futile is the fear that the Liberals are about to propose "the impossible." There is nothing in politics to which that word can be applied, as even the most cursory study of our history will show. When men say that certain measures can "never" be carried, they are more likely to be wrong than right. In 1687 it would have been deemed impossible to place the Crown upon a strictly parliamentary basis ; in 1689 this was accomplished. In 1830 the most sanguine reformer scarcely dared hope that borough-mongering would in his lifetime be destroyed, and the first popularly elected Parliament was chosen in 1832. In 1865, none could have dreamed that household suffrage in the boroughs was near ; in 1867 it was adopted by a Tory Government. In 1867 he would have been a hardy prophet who would have foretold the speedy downfall of the Irish Episcopal Establishment ; and the Act of Disestablishment was placed upon the statute book in 1869. Such instances should of a surety teach men to be modest in their forecasts of what is possible in politics.

In, therefore, pursuing our search into the why and the wherefore of the politics of the future, we must put aside phrases and come to facts. The phrases will die, but the facts will remain ; and the more closely we grasp these latter the more certain will those Liberal principles which have done so much for the past, do even more for the future.

And, when we come to the facts, we must not forget that a political question is not necessarily unpractical because it cannot be immediately dealt with ; for good is accomplished by the calm discussion of points which are bound some time to be raised, and which, if undebated now, may be settled in a gust of popular passion. As Mr. John Morley has well observed—"The fact that leading statesmen are of necessity so absorbed in the tasks of the hour furnishes all the better reason why as many other people as possible should busy themselves in helping to prepare opinion for the practical application of unfamiliar but weighty and promising suggestions, by constant and ready discussion of them upon their merits."

# X.—SHOULD HOME RULE BE GRANTED TO IRELAND?

THE question of Irish self-government is for the present the greatest that concerns the Liberal party, and in current politics, as Mr. Gladstone has truly and tersely put it, Ireland blocks the way. This, of course, is not so simply because Mr. Gladstone said it, and even less is it so because he wished it. The question stands in the path of all other great measures of legislative reform, for the sufficient reason that, at the first opportunity after the franchise was enjoyed by every householder, Ireland declared emphatically, and by a majority unparalleled in modern political history, in favour of freedom to manage her own domestic affairs.

It must be obvious that, when all the popularly-elected members for three out of four provinces into which one of the countries which form this kingdom is divided, pronounce against the existing system of government, and when a majority of those for the other province side with them, that that system cannot continue to exist with the good will of those whom it most intimately affects, and can only be maintained by force. Such as have followed Mr. Gladstone in this matter do not believe in the maintenance of a government against the constitutionally declared will of the governed, and are agreed that the Irish demand for the management of purely domestic affairs ought to be granted on the grounds of justice, expediency, and sound Liberal principles.

They hold that to grant the demand would be just, because under the present system the vast majority of Irishmen have no practical control over those by whom they are governed ; that it would be expedient, because the kingdom is weakened by the continual disaffection of one of its component parts ; and that it would accord with sound Liberal principles, in that the overwhelming majority of the Irish electorate have asked for Home Rule through the constitutional medium of the ballot-box.

" The liberty of a people," says Cowley, " consists in being governed by laws which they have made themselves, under whatever form it be of government." This definition, which applies strictly to England, applies not at all to Ireland. The English system of government has broken down there so completely that all parties profess to be agreed that something must be devised in its place. Liberals have always held that a people or a class knows better what is good for it than any other people or any other class, however enlightened or well-meaning. That has been one of the main reasons for giving the suffrage to the poor, the ignorant, and the helpless, because the experience of ages has taught that the rich, the educated, and the powerful, while well able to take care of themselves, are either too careless or have too little knowledge to take the same care of others. And as with the suffrage, so with self-government. Any extension must be granted upon broad principles : small concessions grudgingly given are always accepted without gratitude, and used to extort greater.

" Well," it may be said, " I am willing to give Ireland a large measure of self-government, but I won't yield to agitators." This is one of the oldest of all replies to demands for reform. How could anything be gained in politics without agitation ? The Tories swear they will yield nothing until agitation has ceased ; and if it ceases, if only for a moment, they declare it is evident there is no popular wish for reform. " Proceed, my lords," said Lord Mansfield, when the American colonies revolted—" proceed, my lords, with spirit and firmness ; and when you shall have established your authority, it will then be time to show lenity." And their lordships proceeded ; but the " time to show lenity " never came, for it was such counsels which lost the American colonies to the British Crown.

" But," it will be added, " this is not an ordinary agitation ; it is a revolutionary one." In some of its phases that is true, and it is all the more reason why its cause should be closely examined. It is the English themselves who have taught the Irish that ordinary constitutional agitation gains them nothing. If it had not been for the organization of the Volunteers, Grattan's Parliament of 1782 would never have been granted ; the Duke of Wellington in 1829 admitted that he yielded Catholic Emancipation to the threat of civil war; it needed the terrible crimes of the early "thirties" to arouse England to the necessity for abolishing an iniquitous system of levying tithe ; the Fenian outbreaks, the attack on a prison van at Manchester, and the blowing up of a gaol in London, opened the eyes of the English to the need for disestablishing the Irish Church and clipping the claws of the Irish landlords ; the fearful winter of 1880 led to the granting of still further protection to the tenants ; and to the "plan of campaign" of the winter of 1886 was it owing that a Tory Government felt compelled to still further encroach upon the property and privileges of the landlords of Ireland. As long as Ireland has held to constitutional agitation—as witness that for Catholic Emancipation from 1801 to 1825, and that for tenant right from 1850 to 1868—so long has England refused to grant a single just demand ; and this is exactly what the Tories are doing now. Is it any wonder that Irish agitation should have become revolutionary when that is the only kind we have rewarded ? In the relations between the governing classes and popular movements there has all through been this difference— in England, revolution has been staved off by reform ; in Ireland, reform has been staved off till there was revolution.

"But," it may be continued, " it is not so much that the agitation is revolutionary as that it is criminal which makes me object." But a movement ought not to be called criminal because of the excesses of a few of its extreme partisans. No great popular agitation has ever been free from lewd fellows of the baser sort, who have given occasion to the enemy to blaspheme. But did English Liberals hesitate to support Mazzini because he was accused of favouring assassination ; to sympathize with the French Republicans because Orsini prepared bombs for the destruction of Napoleon III. ; or to-day to wish well to those

Russians who conspire for liberty because the wilder spirits among them have assassinated one Czar and attempted to assassinate another? In our own history, are the Covenanters to be condemned because some of them murdered Archbishop Sharpe ; the early Radicals because Thistlewood and his fellows plotted to kill King and Cabinet ; the Reformers of 1831 because of the Bristol riots and the destruction of Nottingham Castle ; or those of 1866 because the Hyde Park railings were thrown down? When it is remembered that even such a man as Peel could, in the midst of a heated controversy, accuse such another as Cobden of conniving at assassination, we should be careful how we accept the testimony of any partisan concerning the criminality of an agitation to which he is opposed.

These objections touch, after all, only the fringe of the matter, and another which is frequently urged—that the Irish agitation is a "foreign conspiracy" because it receives aid from the United States—does not go much closer to the root. But this, like the others, may be disposed of by English examples. Did not Englishmen aid, both by men and money, in liberating Greece and uniting Italy? Did they not help by subscriptions the insurrections in Hungary and Poland, and, when the former failed, did not many of them take the refugees into their homes? Did they not even raise a fund to assist the slave-holding States when in rebellion? And in all these cases, except in a remote degree the last, they had no tie in blood, but only one in sympathy, with those concerned. That the Nationalist movement has been largely aided from the United States is undoubted ; but that aid has mainly come from those of Irish birth or parentage who have been driven across the Atlantic to seek a home. And when it is said that, because of this help, a self-governed Ireland would rely upon the United States to the detriment of England, may we not ask why it is that Italy does not rely upon France, though it was France that struck the first effective blow for Italian unity ; or Bulgaria upon Russia, though without the blood-sacrifice of Russia that principality would never have occupied a place on the European map? However much it may be to be regretted, gratitude does not play any large part in international affairs.

When the more serious objections to the granting of Home Rule are urged they are no more difficult to meet. " Ireland is not a nation,",it is said ; " its people are of different races." The argument has been used before by the Tories, and the value of it may be judged by an example. The late Lord Derby, as leader of the Tory party, addressed the House of Lords in 1860 in savage denunciation of the efforts then being made to secure the unity of Italy ; and to the contention that all the inhabitants of that peninsula were Italians, he answered, in the words of *Macbeth* to his hired murderers,

> Aye, in the catalogue ye go for men ;
> As hounds and greyhounds, mongrels, spaniels, curs,
> Shoughs, water-rugs, and demi-wolves are cleped
> All by the name of dogs.

And those who remember the unbridgeable differences which then appeared to exist between the Sardinian and the Sicilian, the Florentine and the Neapolitan, the dweller in Venice and the resident in Rome, will know that the perfect unity between them which now makes Italy one of the Great Powers would have been considered as unlikely as any between a Belfast man and an inhabitant of Cork to-day.

" The Irish are not fit for self-government," is the next contention. If this be so, the shame is ours in not having given them the opportunity for being trained. We did not refuse to liberate the slaves until they were proved to be fit for freedom ; we did not decline to give the labourers the suffrage until they were proved to be capable of rightly using it ; for we knew in each case that no such proof could be afforded until the opportunity was offered. No proof that the Irish are not able to manage a Parliament is given by the corruption of the semi-independent body which they enjoyed from 1782 to 1799 ; for that consisted entirely of Protestants, mainly chosen by a band of boroughmongers, whom Pitt had to buy out at a high price. The same thing exactly was said by the Tories—sneers about the pigs and all—of the Bulgarians in 1876 ; and they have had good reason since to change their minds. What reason is there to believe that the Irish would be less able to manage their own affairs than the people of Bulgaria?

"But they are naturally lawless." Where is the proof? It is true that in certain mountainous districts of Kerry and Clare there have been outbursts of moonlighting, but these have been as nothing compared with the prevalence of brigandage in Greece before the Greeks were allowed to rule themselves, or in Italy before the Italians founded their united kingdom. Where there is little popular respect for the law, there lawlessness flourishes ; where the people make their own laws, there lawlessness is put down with a strong hand.

"If they had the power they would persecute the Protestants." This is a prophecy, and a prophet has the advantage of being able to soar above proofs. But the fact that every prominent defender of national rights in Ireland for the last century and a half, except O'Connell, from Dean Swift down to Mr. Parnell, has been a Protestant, should count for something. The fact that Protestants have again and again been returned to the Corporations of the most Catholic cities should count for much. And the fact that, when for years not a single one of the 450 English members was a Roman Catholic, several of the 103 Irish members, even from the most Catholic districts, were Protestants, should count for more. Such religious persecution as exists in Ireland is certainly more at Belfast than at Cork.

"Giving them a Parliament would break up the empire." Why should the empire be broken up because there was extended to Ireland the principle we have granted to Australia and Canada, New Zealand and the Cape? How is it that the German Empire continues united, though the Reichstag, its Imperial Parliament, is one body, and the Prussian Parliament, the Saxon Parliament, the Würtemberg Parliament, and the Bavarian Parliament are quite others? Is there no union between Austria and Hungary, or between Sweden and Norway, though each has its Parliament, and are the United States disintegrated because every one of the States has its own Senate and House of Representatives? If one were asked to name two of the strongest nations outside our own, Germany and the United States would be the reply; and in each there is a system of Home Rule for the separate portions.

"But did not the United States crush the Confederates when secession was demanded?" Of course they did; the United States fought against the South separating from the North, as we should against Ireland separating from England. But every State which joined the Confederacy possessed as ample a measure of Home Rule as the Liberals now propose for Ireland; and, to the lasting honour of the Northern States, that measure was restored soon after the war. Home Rule the South had, and has still; separation the South asked for, and did not receive.

"The Irish are ungrateful people; whatever you give them they ask for more." Would it not be well to first ask what the Irish have had to be grateful for? Granting that we yielded Catholic Emancipation, reformed the tithe system, disestablished the Church, and legalized tenant right; why, after all these things, should we expect gratitude? The old phrase that "gratitude is a lively sense of favours to come" may be unduly cynical; but is it not absurd to ask that recompense for the doing of acts of simple justice? Former generations of Englishmen deprived the Irish of their rights. To what thanks are later generations entitled for simply restoring to the Irish the rights of which they had been robbed? "Be just and fear, not," was said of ancient time: "Be just and expect not gratitude," should be added to-day. And when it is stated that "the Irish ought to accept what we choose to give them," it must be replied that this is the purely despotic argument which has already done England sufficient injury by losing her the United States.

It is only in this, the briefest, fashion that an answer has been sketched to the various arguments and assumptions against Home Rule. In determining to grant it, the Liberals are acting strictly according to their old policy of favouring struggling nationalities. The support given by Burke to the cause of America; by Fox to Ireland; by Canning (in this, as in some other matters, truly Liberal) to Greece; by Palmerston to Italy; and by Mr. Gladstone to Bulgaria, indicates with sufficient clearness the traditional Liberal position. For a century we have been telling the whole world the advantages of autonomy;

are we now to decline to adopt, in similar circumstances, the remedy for discontent we have all along preached to, and sometimes forced upon, others?

The Liberals say with Landor, "Let us try rather to remove the evils of Ireland than to persuade those who undergo them that there are none." They are utterly opposed to the idea that it is right to give a people free representation and then deliberately to ignore all that that representation asks. They are, it is true, in a minority at this moment, but they do not forget that all great causes have three stages—first to be laughed at, next to be looked at, and last to be loved. Home Rule has certainly reached the second stage; it will soon reach the third. The Liberals have been beaten before, but they have always won in the end. And it is well to be beaten sometimes. If life were all sunshine we should find it oppressive; an occasional cloud serves to temper the heat. To the Liberals, as to nature itself, a misty morning is often the prelude to the brightest day.

# XI.—WHAT SHOULD BE DONE WITH THE LORDS?

In dealing with the other questions which the Liberals will have to consider, it will be well to take them in what may be called their constitutional order, and a beginning, therefore, may be made with the reform of the House of Lords. The theory upon which that House is upheld is that it is an assembly of our most notable men, called to rule either by descent from the great ones of the past, or by the proved capacity of themselves in the present, who discuss every question laid before them with impartiality, and who act as a check upon the hasty and ill-considered legislation of the House of Commons.

So much for the theory : what of the fact? Those peers who are not creations of to-day mainly spring either from Pitt's plutocrats or from those who have been granted their patents because of having lavishly spent their money in electoral support of some party ; those who can claim their peerage by direct descent from the great ones of the past can be numbered by tens, while the whole body is numbered by hundreds ; and just as a sprinkling of successful lawyers, soldiers, and brewers adds nothing to its historical character, it in no sense brings the peerage into clear and close contact with the people. As to the impartiality displayed by the House of Lords, it is notorious that in these days it is little other than an appanage of the Carlton Club, and that, whatever the Tory whips desire it to do, it accomplishes without demur. And its power as a check upon hasty and ill-considered legislation may be judged from the fact that it never dares reject a measure which public opinion strongly demands and upon which the Commons insist.

When the history of the House of Lords is studied, it will be found that during the past century it has initiated no great measure for the public good, and a hundred times has wantonly mutilated or impotently opposed the reforms the people asked. The mischief it has done touches every department of public life. Whether it was to throw out a bill abolishing the penalty of death for stealing in a shop to the value of five shillings, on the ground stated by one of the bishops in the majority that it was "too speculative to be safe ; " to again and again vote down every proposal to relieve Roman Catholics and Jews from civil disabilities; to pander to the will of George IV. in the prolonged persecution of his wife ; or to defeat measures calculated to place the electoral power in the hands of the people—the House of Lords has always been one of the main forces in the army of darkness and oppression. Remember that every one of the reforms the Liberals have secured within the last 50 years has been distasteful to the House of Lords, and calculate the worth or wisdom of that institution.

It does not add to the estimation of either the worth or the wisdom that the Lords have ultimately accepted what they have bitterly opposed, for if they have consistently been a stumbling-block in the path of every reform which the people now cherish their tardy repentance is of little avail as long as they pursue the same obstructive course. And it is not merely measures which they throw out, but measures which they mutilate, that render them a power for harm. For the Lords are like rabbits ; it is not so much what they swallow as what they spoil which makes them so destructive.

Those who defend the institution as it exists should, therefore, be called upon to point to some one definite case in recent history in which it can be said, " Here has the House of Lords done good." Mere talk about the admirable administrators and the dexterous debaters it contains is no argument ; for if the legislative functions of the peers were abolished to-morrow, those among them who were worthy a seat in the House of Commons would have no difficulty in securing it. What Liberals object to is the being subjected to the caprices, the passions, and the prejudices of some five hundred men, the majority of whom are not merely unskilled in legislative faculty and unqualified in administrative experience, but are drawn from a single class out of touch and sympathy with the mass of the people.

It is not the least of the evils of the present system that the attendance at the sittings of the Lords is of so perfunctory a nature. Even during the discussion of important measures not more than sixty or seventy peers, out of over five hundred, are commonly present, while ten or twelve is not an unusual number to deal with Bills. As Erskine May has pointed out, " Three peers may wield all the authority of the House. Nay, even less than that number are competent to pass or reject a law, if their unanimity should avert a division, on notice of their imperfect constitution." And he furnishes an instance where an Irish Land Bill, " which had occupied weeks of discussion in the Commons, was nearly lost by a disagreement between the two Houses, the numbers, on a division, being seven and six."

Adding to their number does not improve the average attendance, and yet the pace at which that number is growing is a scandal. In 1885, for the first time since 1832, the total membership of the House of Commons was enlarged, not without trepidation and despite the fact that every member would be directly responsible to a constituency. The increase was only twelve, and a Premier often creates within a year as many legislators on his own account, who, with their successors, are responsible to no one for their public conduct. Is it not an absurdity to speak of ourselves as freely governed and ruled only by our own consent when a Prime Minister can make as many legistators as he chooses, and there be none to gainsay him?

If it were only that under the present system the drunken and the dissolute, the blackleg and the debauchee are allowed to sit in the Lords and make laws for us and our children, we should have a right to demand that the institution should be " mended or ended." The former process has now distinctly been adopted as a plank in the Liberal platform, and the question of reform can, therefore, no longer be put on one side.

There are many Radicals who say that as the House of Lords, if it agrees with the Commons, is useless, and if it disagrees is dangerous, its abolition as a legislative body should at once be made a plank in the party programme. They argue further, that to reform will be to strengthen it, and that, by the reasoning just given, this is undesirable. But the main point is to secure the best legislative machine we can, and there is much to be said for the improvement of the House of Lords into a Senate which shall be in fact what the present institution is in theory—a body of sage statesmen, experienced in affairs, and elected for a specified term, so as to be directly amenable to the people, and not removed from obedience to public opinion.

As a first step to any reform, the creation of hereditary peerages, conferring a power to legislate, ought to be stopped. " The tenth transmitter of a foolish face " ought no longer to be able to transmit with the foolishness a power over the lives and liberties of his fellow-men. If there is any one who continues honestly to believe that because a man has secured a peerage by his brains (and the proportion of creations upon that ground is exceeding small) his successors are likely to prove good legislators, he would do well to procure a list of those peers who are descended from " law lords ; " and he would find that while not one of them is distinguished for great political or administrative skill, there are various notorious instances, which will occur to every reader of the daily newspaper, of those distinguished for exactly the reverse.

One minor reform in the constitution of the House of Lords ought to be pressed at once, and that is the removal of the bishops from their present place within it. Not only has no one section of religious persons the right to a State-created ascendency over others, but all parties are agreed in the most practical form that bishops as bishops have no inherent right to legislative power. In 1847, when the bishopric of Manchester was created, it was provided that the junior member of the episcopal bench for the time being should not have a seat in the Lords, and thirty years later, when the Government of Lord Beaconsfield made further new bishoprics, it similarly did not venture to add to the number of spiritual peers ; there are consequently always four or five waiting outside the gilded chamber until the death of their seniors shall let them in.

What Liberals, therefore, demand is that the House of Lords shall be thoroughly reformed. The bishops must be excluded, no more hereditary legislators created, and a system devised by which the House shall become a Senate so chosen as to be directly responsible to the people, whose interests it is assumed to serve. A sprinkling of life peers would aggravate instead of lessen the difficulty. An hereditary legislator may, for the sake of his successors, be careful not too grievously to offend the people ; an elected legislator, for his own sake, will be the same ; but a legislator who was neither one nor the other would have no such check, and all experience has shown that corporations elected for life become cliquish or even corrupt, for want of the frequent and wholesome breeze of public opinion.

# XII.—IS THE HOUSE OF COMMONS PERFECT?

THERE was a time, and that not far distant, when the question "Is the House of Commons perfect?" would have been considered by many well-intentioned and easy-going persons to be impertinent, even if not actually irreverent. But we live in days when every institution has to submit to the test of free discussion, and its usefulness and efficiency have to be proved, if it is to retain its place in the political system. And as there can be little doubt that, for many reasons, a feeling has been widely growing within the past few years that the House of Commons is neither as useful nor as efficient as it ought to be, the popular reverence for that great assembly has somewhat diminished; and it behoves all who wish to preserve parliamentary government in its fullest and freest form to examine the causes of apparent decay and to suggest methods of amelioration.

The preservation intact of the powers and privileges of the House of Commons must be the desire of every lover of freedom; but the conduct of its business must be brought into harmony with modern methods, and the mechanical side of the assembly made as perfect as possible. Not from me will fall one word derogatory to the venerable "mother of free parliaments." The House of Commons has done too much for England, its example has done too much for liberty the wide world through, to allow any but the ribald and the unthinking to speak lightly of its history or scornfully of its achievements. For the People's Chamber is not merely the most powerful portion of the High Court of Parliament; it is not alone the central force of the British Constitution, to which kings and nobles have had, and may again have, to bow; it is the directly elected body before whose gaze every wrong can be displayed, and to whose power even the humblest can look for redress. It deals forth justice to the myriad millions of India as to a solitary injured Englishman; it is a sounding board which echoes the claims of a single peasant or an entire people; and it practically commands the issues of peace and war, involving the fate of thousands, and of life and death, involving that of only one. No policy is vast beyond its conception, no person insignificant beyond its sight. It is a mighty engine of freedom, responsive to the heart-throbs and aspirations of a whole people, which has baffled tyrants, liberated slaves, and raised England to that position among the nations which our children and our children's children should be proud to maintain.

Such is the assemby which needs reform. Often enough and with much success has there been raised a cry for " parliamentary reform," but this has meant an amendment of the method of electing members, not of the manner of conducting business; and it is this latter which now is urgently required. The stately ship which has sailed the ocean of public affairs for six centuries has naturally attracted weeds and barnacles which cling to its hull and retard its progress. These must be swept away if the vessel is to pursue a safe and speedy course; and as little irreverence is involved in the process as in cleaning and repairing the old *Victory* herself.

The cardinal defect of the existing system is that it strives to do modern work by ancient modes, an attempt which is as certain to fail in public concerns as it would be if any one were sufficiently ill-advised to try it in private. And when there is contemplated on the one side the vast and growing mass of affairs cast upon the consideration of Parliament, and on the other the rusty and creaking machinery employed to cope with it, little wonder can be felt that much needful work is left undone, and a deal of that which is accomplished is done badly.

By granting to Ireland the right to manage **her** domestic

affairs, and by providing some system by which England, Scotland, and Wales can in local assemblies each deal for herself with her own concerns, much will be accomplished in the way of real parliamentary reform. But even then more will remain to be done. The multiplied stages of each measure laid before the House of Commons must be lessened. It is possible to-day to have a debate and a division upon the motion for leave to introduce a bill, upon the first reading, the second reading, the proposal to go into committee, the report stage, the third reading, and the final proposition " That the bill do pass," while financial bills have even more stages to go through ; and although, of course, all these opportunities for almost unlimited obstruction are not often made use of, they exist and should be diminished.

Another fruitful source of wasted parliamentary time is the provision that if a bill is dropped at the end of a session, however far it may have progressed short of actual passing, it has to be started afresh when the House re-assembles, and every stage has to be as laboriously again gone through as if the measure had never been heard of before. One can understand why a new Parliament should start with a clean sheet, for no decision of a previous one in favour of the principle of a certain measure can bind it to pass that measure into law. But within the limits of the same Parliament, a decision once given should be so far binding that it should not be necessary for a bill to pass the stage of second reading four or five years running, because effluxion of time had prevented it passing into law during any of the sessions.

Against such waste of time as this—waste which is imposed by the very rules under which Parliament works—the closure is no remedy. It is a weapon with which it is right that the majority should be armed, but it requires great skill in the wielding lest the legitimate efforts of the minority be stifled. What is wanted is the better ordering of the whole machine. When private bills and purely local business are taken elsewhere, when the stages of each measure are lessened, and when bills which have passed their second reading are not killed at the session's end, but allowed to remain in a state of animated expectancy, even then other means will have to be sought to make the machine move more surely and with greater expedition.

Something has been done to this end by the earlier hour of assembling and fixed hour of adjourning which the House has now adopted. But why should not the process be carried further, and the affairs of the country be settled by day instead of by night ? The first answer is that it would not be possible for a legislative body to do its business during the day ; and a sufficient answer should be that the French Assembly and the German Reichsrath do theirs during that period. The next is that Ministers could not get through their work if the hours of meeting were made earlier ; the reply is to the same effect— that what French and German Ministers can accomplish, English Ministers must be taught to do. A further contention is that such barristers and business men as are members would not be able to attend sooner than at present ; and the answer of many as to the barristers would be that it were well for the country if three-fourths of those in the House never attended at all, for it is largely owing to the number of lawyers in Parliament that the law is a complicated and costly process, often proving an engine of injustice in the hands of the rich, and a ruinous remedy for the injured poor ; while as to the business men who cannot attend earlier than now, their number is so exceedingly limited that their convenience ought not to be consulted to the detriment of parliamentary institutions. There is one more argument which would be of greater weight than all the rest if present conditions were likely to continue, and that is, that it would be a serious hindrance to private bill legislation, because members would be loth to serve on committees during the time the House was deliberating ; but it is obvious to all observers of the parliamentary machine that the greater portion of private business will have soon to be delegated to other bodies, and the main point of an undeniably strong argument will thus be destroyed.

But even such a reform in the hours of work would not expedite matters to a sufficient extent, if the present power of unlimited talk be preserved. Every member has the right of speaking once at each stage of a bill, and as many times as he likes during committee. If the number of stages be lessened, as they are likely to be, there will not be much to be objected to in the continuance of this right ; but its retention should be contingent upon the shortening of each speech. This is a proposal which can be justified on "plain Whig principles," and has certainly a plain Whig precedent. For Lord John Russell, when Prime Minister, brought forward in 1849 a proposal to limit the duration of all speeches to one hour, except in the case of a member introducing an original motion, or a minister of the Crown speaking in reply. The proposal fell through, but that it was made by so cautious a Premier is a proof that there is much to be said in favour of compulsorily shortening speeches.

The proposition that Parliaments should be chosen more frequently in order that they may preserve a closer touch with the people should be earnestly pressed forward. In the early days of the House of Commons annual Parliaments were practically the rule, an assembly being summoned to vote supplies and do certain necessary business and then dissolved. When matters were put upon a more certain footing, after the Great Rebellion, Parliaments elected for three years were ordained, and this term was extended to seven years shortly after the Hanoverian Accession, in order to guard against a Jacobite success at the hustings, which might seriously have endangered an unstable throne. The time has now come to ask that a term adopted in a panic, and for reasons which have long passed away, should be shortened. A four years' Parliament has been found to be long enough for France, Germany. and the United States ; and as the average of the last half-century has proved a seven years' period to be unnecessarily long for England. the briefer should be enacted. Now that the suffrage is on so wide a basis. it is essential that members of Parliament should be in as close touch with the people as possible. Once elected. members frequently forget that they are not the masters of those who have chosen them, and that, though called in one sense to rule the country, there is another sense in which they are called to serve. It is necessary that this truth should be enforced upon such members as are apt to ignore it, and shorter Parliaments would enforce it.

There are some who believe that by payment of members a better representation of the people would be secured. The example of other countries can certainly be quoted in favour of such a proposition, but there appears no necessity for any general payment in England. As, however, it is in the highest degree desirable that representatives of every class in the community should appear at Westminster, some provision should be made by which members, upon making a statutory declaration of the necessity for such a course, would be able to claim a certain moderate allowance for their expenses during the session. There would be nothing revolutionary in this ; the fact of members being paid would be merely a return to the practice which prevailed for close upon four centuries after the House of Commons was established upon its present basis.

# XIII.—IS OUR ELECTORAL SYSTEM COM-PLETE ?

MANY would be surprised if told that there remained serious deficiencies in our electoral system ; and would ask, " How can that be ? We now have the ballot at elections, household suffrage in both counties and boroughs, and a nearer approach to equal electoral districts than the most sanguine Radical ten or even five years ago would have thought possible ? "

But has the suffrage really been extended to every house-holder ? As a fact, it has not ; it is largely a merely nominal extension ; and tens of thousands of qualified citizens are dis-franchised for years at a time by the needless restrictions and petty technicalities which now clog the electoral law. Registra-tion should be so simplified that every qualified person would be certain of finding his name on the list ; and the duty of com-piling a correct register should be imposed upon some local public official, compelled under penalty to perform it.

The common belief is that a twelvemonth's occupation qualifies for a vote, but all that it does is to qualify for a place on the register, which is an altogether different matter, the register being made up months before it comes into operation. At the very least, a man must have gone into a house a year and a half before he has a vote for it, and it often happens that he has to be in it for two years and a quarter, and even more, before he possesses the franchise. Let me state such a case. A man goes into a house at the half-quarter in August, 1888 ; he will not be entitled to be placed on the register in the autumn of 1889, because he was not occupying on July 15 of the previous year ; if he continues to occupy, he will, however, be placed there in the autumn of 1890 ; but it is not until January 1, 1891, that he will be able to exercise the suffrage. So that all taking houses from July 15, 1888, are in the same position as those who take them up to July 15, 1889, and will have to wait for a vote until 1891.

" But," it may be said, " when a man once has his vote he is able to retain it as long as he holds any dwelling by virtue of ' successive occupation.' " That is so only as long as he remains within the boundaries of the constituency wherein he possessed the original qualification. He may move from one division of Liverpool to another, or from one division of Manchester to another, or from one division of Birmingham to another, and retain his vote by successive occupation : but if he goes from Liverpool to Birkenhead, from Manchester to Salford, or from Birmingham to Aston, his vote is lost for the year and a half or the two years and a quarter before explained. The effect of this is most apparent in London, where thousands of working men are continually moving from one district to another, treating the whole metropolis as one great town, but by passing out of their original borough they are disfranchised. And this is the more a grievance because the Redistribution Act, though dividing the larger provincial towns into single-member districts, left them as boroughs intact ; while the old constituencies in London were not merely divided, but split up into separate boroughs. Lambeth thus became three boroughs—Lambeth, Camberwell, and Newington — each with its own divisions; Hackney was severed into the boroughs of Hackney, Shoreditch, and Bethnal Green ; Marylebone into the boroughs of Marylebone, Paddington, St. Pancras, and Hampstead ; and so throughout the metropolis. And the consequence of the purely artificial nature of the boundary lines thus created is that many a man who merely moves from one side of the street to the other, or even from one house to another next door, is disfranchised for a couple of years. The obvious remedy for this peculiar evil is that London should be treated as one single borough, like Liverpool, Manchester, and Birmingham ; but the remedy for the whole evil is that when a man has once qualified for a place on the register, proof of successive occupation in any part of the country should suffice to give him his vote in the constituency to which he moves.

When we pass from the household to the lodger franchise, we are faced by one of the hugest shams in the electoral system. There are certain constituencies which contain hundreds of lodgers, and of these not more than tens are on the register. The reason is twofold : it is not merely a trouble to get a vote, but there is a yearly difficulty in retaining it. For a lodger, as for a household vote, a twelvemonth's occupation is necessary to qualify, and the purely nominal nature of this qualification is the same in both ; but the lodger has the additional hardship of being deprived of even as much benefit as "successive occupation" gives the householder, for if he moves next door, though with the same landlord, he is disfranchised, while the landlord retains his vote. And, further, he has to make a formal claim for the suffrage every succeeding summer, an operation too troublesome for the vast majority of lodgers to undergo, and one from which the householder is spared. And thus this particular franchise is a mockery, and the proportion of lodger voters to qualified lodgers is absurdly small.

Of course, the term "householder," equally with the term "lodger," presupposes at present that the one who bears it is a man, and, equally of course, an agitation is on foot to give the franchise to women. This is a matter which is likely to be settled in favour of the other sex, and the only question is as to how far it should go. The extreme advocates of female suffrage would give it to married women, but what appears the growing opinion is that spinsters and widows, qualified for the suffrage as men are qualified, should receive it ; and this is a settlement which will probably soon be reached.

Much dissatisfaction would continue to be felt, even were these points granted, if "faggot-voting" were still suffered, or a single person allowed to possess a multitude of votes. The "forty-shilling freehold" is a prolific source of bogus qualifications : abolished in Ireland by the Tories because it gave the people too much power, it ought to be got rid of throughout the

kingdom by the Liberals because it leaves the people too little.
For it is largely by its means that some men are able to boast
that they can exercise the franchise in six, or ten, or even a dozen
constituencies. Men of this type occupy themselves at a general
election by travelling around, dropping a vote here and a vote
there, and they ought to be restrained. That this can be done
without violating any right is evident even under the present
system. However many qualifications a man obtains, he can vote
for only one of them in any constituency ; and more, if he has
qualifications in every division of the same borough he has, when
the register is made up, to state for which division he will vote,
and in that division alone can he claim a ballot paper. If it is
right to prevent him from having more than a single vote in any
one division—or, which is a still stronger point, in any one
borough—it must be equally right to limit him to a single vote
throughout the country. "One man, one vote," should be the
rule in a democratic state. If a person possesses qualifications
for various constituencies, let him be called upon to do what he
is now compelled to do if he has qualifications for different parts
of the same constituency—vote for only one of them ; and that
one should be the place in which he habitually resides.

An indirect method of practically securing the "one man, one
vote," result would be to have all the elections throughout the
country on the same day. Under the existing system, the polls
drag on for weeks, and not only does this distract the attention
of the nation and put a hindrance to business for a far longer
period than is necessary, but it has the further evil effect of
causing many voters in the constituencies which are later polled
to waver until they see whither the majority elsewhere are tending, and then "go with the stream." The only instance in
recent electoral history when the later polls reversed the verdict
of the earlier was at the general election of 1885, when the
boroughs, speaking broadly, voted Tory and the counties Liberal ;
but that, owing to the recent extension of the county franchise,
was an abnormal period, and the rule is that the stream gathers
as it goes, and the waverers are swept into the torrent. That it
is possible for a great country to be polled on the same day is
evident from the examples of Germany and France, and it is

only adherence to worn-out forms which prevents its accomplishment here.

The remedy, therefore, for the anomalies caused by the defective "successive occupation," the presence of "faggot voters," and the prolongation of the pollings, is simply to treat the kingdom as one vast constituency, in which a man once on the register remains as long as he has a qualification, in which no one has more than a single vote, and in all the divisions of which the poll is taken on the same day.

This suggested single constituency would, of course, resemble the great county and borough constituencies of to-day in having divisions, but it would not be single in the sense proposed in Mr. Hare's original scheme of "proportional representation," by which the possessor of a vote could cast it where and for whom he liked. Those who have adopted Mr. Hare's ideas, while modifying his methods, have not been successful in discovering any feasible plan for representing public opinion in the proportion in which it is held, the sort of Chinese puzzle proposed by Sir John Lubbock and Mr. Courtney having failed to commend itself to any practical politician. It is wrong, however, to imagine that the present system of single-member districts roughly secures that the minority shall be duly represented while the majority retains its due share of power ; for it was proved in some striking instances, the very first time it was put in operation, that, so far from retaining, it often sacrifices the rights of the majority. At the general election of 1885 the Liberals of Leeds cast 23,354 votes, and the Tories 19,605, and yet the latter gained three seats and the former only two ; the Sheffield Liberals won but two seats with 19,636 votes, while the Tories secured three with 19,594 ; and the Hackney Liberals could win only one seat with 9,203 votes, and the Tories two with 8,870 ; while, on the other side, the Southwark Tories, with 9,324 votes, returned one member, and the Liberals, with 9,120, returned two. The reason is obvious : a party with overwhelming majorities in one or two districts is liable to be beaten by narrow majorities in most of the divisions, and the minority thus elects a majority of members. The present system, therefore, is evidently imperfect. It was adopted in haste and without due discussion ; it has failed in France, Switzerland, and the United States ; and in at least the divided boroughs it ought to give place to double or triple member districts.

The question of having second ballots, so as to provide that, as in Germany and France, where there are several candidates and none secures an absolute majority of votes given, another ballot shall be held, is not an immediately pressing one, though much may be said in its favour ; but that of the payment of election expenses out of the rates ought to be dealt with at once.  It is highly unfair that a candidate should be fined heavily, by the enforced payment of the official expenses, for his desire to serve the country in Parliament ; and it is the more unfair because the official expenses of elections for town councils, school boards, and boards of health and of guardians are paid by the public.

This fine helps to keep men of moderate means out of the House, though their abilities might prove to be most useful there ; and another method by which the wealthy have the advantage in parliamentary contests ought equally to be attended to.  People are forbidden by law to hire conveyances for carrying voters to the poll, but they are allowed to borrow them, with the result that constituencies on an election day swarm with carriages of peers and other rich people, who have nothing whatever to do with the district, and who yet affect by this influence the voting.  The use of carriages should not be prohibited, for the aged and infirm ought not to be disfranchised ; but no importation of vehicles should be allowed, and while an elector, and an elector only, should be entitled to use his own, it should, as a means of identification, be driven by himself.  Such a provision would largely diminish the present interference of peers in elections.  They may address as many meetings as they like ; but, as long as they have a legislative assembly of their own, they must not be allowed to use their wealth and position to interfere with the voters for the Commons House of Parliament.

# XIV.—SHOULD THE CHURCH REMAIN ESTABLISHED?

FROM the great concerns of the State it is natural to come to the Church, and when that point is arrived at, the problem of disestablishment at once arises. " *Can* the Church be disestablished?" is a question sometimes put, and the answer is plain, for that answer is "Most certainly," and a further question " Where is the Act establishing the Church?" as if the non-production of such an enactment would prevent Parliament from severing the link which binds Church and State, may be replied to by another. Supposing one asked, " Where is the Act establishing the monarchy?" would the non-production of that measure prove that it is not a parliamentary monarchy under which we live? By the Act of Succession, Parliament " settled " the monarchy; by various Acts in the reigns of Henry VIII., Edward VI., Elizabeth, and Charles II., Parliament has " settled " the Church. There is no authority in this realm higher than Parliament; and if Parliament chooses to "unsettle "either monarchy or Church, it can do so.

This is no new-fangled Radical idea; it is an old Whig principle. Charles Fox, in a debate just a century since, observed, while favourable to the principle of religious establishments, "If the majority of the people of England should ever be for the abolition of the Established Church, in such a case the abolition ought immediately to follow." Macaulay, in his essay on Mr. Gladstone's youthful book on " Church and State," was clearly of the same opinion. And Lord Hartington, in his declaration a few years ago that if the majority of the people of Scotland desired disestablishment their desire ought to be satisfied, completed the chain of Whig traditional opinion.

If upon such a matter one is not content to swear by the Whigs, the verdict of the bishops may be accepted. Dr. Magee, of Peterborough, has declared that "Our Church is not only catholic and national : she is established by law—that is to say, she has entered into certain definite relations with the State, involving on the part of the State an amount of recognition and control, and on the part of the Church subjection to the State."

The very use of the common term " The Church of England as by law established " involves recognition of the fact that what the law has done the law can undo. And if any one doubts the power of Parliament in this matter, let him read a table of the statutes passed in the session of 1869, and he will find that the most important of all of them was " An Act to put an end to the Establishment of the Church of Ireland." Now, the legal position of the Irish Establishment and the English Establishment was identical. Is any further proof required that, if Parliament chooses, the latter can at any moment be severed from the State?

It is sometimes said that Nonconformist bodies are equally established with the Church because they are subject to the law, as regards the construction of their trust-deeds, and other matters, of which the courts of justice have occasionally to take cognizance. But that is as if it were argued that all persons who come within the enactments affecting the relations between employer and employed should be considered servants of the Crown as well as those engaged in the government offices. The difference is plain : the law regulates all, the Government employs only some. The Crown appoints the Archbishop of Canterbury, but has no right to choose the President of the Wesleyan Conference ; Parliament can deal with the salaries of the bishops, but cannot touch the stipend of a single Congregational minister.

There being no doubt that, if the people will, the Church can be disestablished, a further question remains, " Ought it to be so dealt with ? " and the reply in the affirmative is based upon the lessons of the past, the experiences of the present, and the possibilities of the future.

The Church, though possessed of every advantage which high position and vast wealth could supply, has failed to be "national" in any true sense of the word. So far from embracing the whole people, it has gradually become but one of many sects ; and, had it not been for the efforts of those who conscientiously dissented from its doctrines and its practice, a great portion of the religious life we see in England to-day would not have existed. Further, and from the time of its settlement on the present basis, it has been the consistent friend to the privileged classes, and foe to any extension of liberties to the mass of the people. In defence of its position and emoluments it has struck many a blow for despotism. The harassing and often bloody persecutions of Nonconformists and Roman Catholics in England and Wales, and of Covenanters and Cameronians in Scotland, were undertaken at its desire and in its defence ; while the hardships and indignities inflicted for centuries upon the Catholics of Ireland were avowedly in support of "the Protestant interest"—a Protestantism of the Establishment, in which the Presbyterians were allowed little share. In its pulpits were found the most eloquent defenders of the English slave trade, which was from them declared to be "in conformity with principles of natural and revealed religion ; " and when Romilly strove to lessen the horrors of the penal code, its bishops again and again came to the rescue of laws the disregard of which for the sanctity of human life can in these days scarcely be conceived. And when it was proposed to give to some extent the government of the country to the people whom it mainly concerned, it was the bishops who threw out the first Reform Bill.

At this present the efforts of the better men within the Establishment are hampered by the State connection. It cannot bring its machinery into harmony with the growing needs of the time without appealing to a Parliament in which orthodox and heterodox, Catholic and Atheist, Jew and Quaker, Unitarian and Agnostic sit side by side, and to which a Hindoo has twice narrowly escaped election. By a Prime Minister dependent upon the will of this body its bishops are chosen; by a Lord Chancellor equally so dependent are many of its ministers appointed. Because of the necessity for going to Parliament for every improvement, little improvement is made. Private patronage is left untouched; the scandal of the sale of livings remains unchecked; criminous clerks are often allowed to escape punishment because of the cumbrous methods now provided; and disobedient clergymen defy their bishops and go to prison rather than conform to discipline, the law which permits persistent insubordination and provides an unfitting penalty remaining unaltered because Parliament has too much to do to attend to the Church.

As to the future, things are likely to be worse instead of better. Then, as now, the connection between State and Church will injure both—the State because it is an injustice to all outside the Establishment that a single sect should be propertied and privileged by Parliament, and the Church because it is as a strong man in chains attempting to walk but only succeeding to painfully hobble.

In how many ways disestablishment would benefit the Church, let Dr. Ryle, Bishop of Liverpool, declare :—" (1) It would doubtless give us more liberty, and enable us to effect many useful reforms. (2) It would bring the laity forward into their rightful position, from sheer necessity. (3) It would give us a real and properly constituted Convocation. (4) It would lead to an increase of bishops, a division of dioceses, and a reconstruction of our cathedral bodies. (5) It would make an end of Crown jobs in the choice of bishops, and upset the whole system of patronage. (6) It would destroy all sinecure offices, and drive all drones out of the ecclesiastical hive. (7) It would enable us to make our worship more elastic, and our ritual better suited to the times." True, the bishop adds that the value of these gains must not be exaggerated; but if disestablishment can do even as much good as this to the Church, it cannot be the bad thing some of its opponents would have us believe.

But it is sometimes urged that if the Church were disestablished, there would be no State recognition of religion, and

England would become un-Christian. Is not this a technical
rather than a real argument? Would the number of Christians
in this country be lessened by a single one if the Church were
deprived of State support? Was not the same thing said when
Jews were admitted to Parliament and Atheists claimed admission? And has England ceased to be Christian because Baron
de Worms is sitting on one side of the Speaker and Mr. Bradlaugh on the other?

A more real argument is that disestablishment would break
up the parochial system; but those who use it impute a dis-
creditable lukewarmness to their own community. Seeing what
the Wesleyans, the Congregationalists, the Baptists, and the
other dissenting denominations have done to spread religion in
every village in England and Wales; what the Free Kirk has
accomplished in Scotland; and what the Roman Catholic
Church has effected in Ireland—and all without a penny of
State endowment, and dependent alone for success upon the
gifts of their members—is it to be believed that the adherents
of the Episcopal Church, among whom are included the
wealthiest men in the country, will permit that institution to
perish for lack of aid? Is not experience all the other way?
Is not that of Ireland in particular a striking testimony to the
wisdom of substituting the voluntary system for State support?
Upon this point the testimony of two Irish Protestant bishops
is abundant proof. The Bishop of Ossory, Ferns, and Leighlin
averred, in 1882, that "no one could look attentively upon our
Church's history during the last ten or twelve years without per-
ceiving that, by the good hand of God upon them, there had
been a decided growth in all that was best and purest and most
important. Never in his recollection had their Church been
more clear or united in her testimony to Christian truth, or
more faithful in every good word and work;" and Lord Plun-
ket, the Archbishop of Dublin, has congratulated his clergy
that disestablishment saved the Church from being involved in
the land agitation, adding, "The very disaster which seemed
most to threaten our downfall has been overruled for good."

The question is likely, however, to be considered a more immediately pressing one for Scotland and Wales than for

England.    In Scotland it is the Presbyterian and not the
Episcopalian form of Christian government which is State
supported ; and the fact that forms so opposed in striking
points of doctrine and practice should be established on the
two sides of the Tweed, is an interesting commentary upon the
system generally.   When the majority of the members for
Scotland demand disestablishment, and press that demand upon
us, it will as assuredly be granted as was the like demand
from Ireland just twenty years ago.   And "the Church of
England in Wales"—supported by a small minority, and never
enjoying the confidence of the body of the people—should
similarly be dealt with, according to the wish of the Welsh parliamentary representatives.

The continued existence of the Church of England as an
establishment is the largest question of all, and it is one which
politicians will have to face, if not this year or next year, yet in
the early years to come.   It is only its continued existence "as
an establishment," which is in dispute, for it would be a slander-
ous imputation upon its sons if it were said that a withdrawal
of State support would cause its collapse as a religious body.
The very strides it has made during the last few years, which
are sometimes urged in its defence, have been made not by
State help but by voluntary effort; and if that voluntary
effort had free scope, the good effect would be greater and
more lasting.

What is wanted is that which Cavour asked, "A Free
Church in a Free State," for both would be benefited by the
process, and particularly the former.   When the late Lord
Beaconsfield was asked why, in the height of Tory reaction,
he made no effort to re-establish the Irish Church, he replied
that there was a difference between cutting off a man's head
and putting it on again.   But the illustration was imperfect,
for it is a strange kind of decapitation which strengthens the
patient ; and that was the effect in Ireland.   And the
Irish Church was not only disestablished but *disendowed.*   In
the mind of the practical politician the two processes are in-
separable.

# XV.—WOULD DISENDOWMENT BE JUST?

The question, "Would disendowment be just?" is admittedly a crucial point to determine when the whole subject comes up for settlement, for there are many defenders of the Establishment who exclaim, "We are quite prepared for the severance of the Church from the State, but only upon condition that she retains her endowments."

But the two concerns cannot be separated. Supposing the Government engaged an officer to perform certain functions, and that, in process of time, finding these functions not fulfilled, it determined to sever the connection, would the officer be justified in demanding not only consideration for his long service and his life interests, but that his salary should be paid to himself and his descendants in perpetuity, though directly neither he nor they would again render service to the State? If it be contended that the illustration is not applicable, because the Church receives no aid from the State, issue can be joined at once.

For what is the first question that naturally arises? It is as to the source from which the Church originally derived her revenues. "Pious benefactors, stimulated by the wish to benefit their fellows and save themselves," is the reply of the average Church defender. But any attempt to prove this fails. Does a solitary person believe that every proprietor of land in each parish of England and Wales voluntarily and spontaneously imposed a tithe upon his possessions? Is it not an admitted fact that it was by royal ordinance such an impost was first levied, and by force of law that it has since been maintained?

This most ancient property of the Church in England, the tithe, is a law-created and law-extorted impost for the benefit of a particular sect. As far back as the Heptarchy, royal ordinances were given in various of the kingdoms of which England was composed directing the payment of tithes ; and that the far greater portion of these were not voluntary offerings is indicated in Hume's account of the West Saxon grant in 854. " Though parishes," he observes, " had been instituted in England by Honorius, Archbishop of Canterbury, two centuries before, the ecclesiastics had never yet been able to get possession of the tithes ; they therefore seized the present favourable opportunity of making that acquisition when a weak, superstitious prince filled the throne, and when the people, discouraged by their losses from the Danes and terrified with the fear of future invasions, were susceptible of any impression which bore the appearance of religion."

When England became one kingdom, and tithes were extended by royal decree to the whole realm, penalties soon began to be provided for non-payment, Alfred ordaining "that if any man shall withhold his tithes, and not faithfully and duly pay them to the Church, if he be a Dane he shall be fined in the sum of twenty shillings, and if an Englishman in the sum of thirty shillings ; " and William the Norman, speedily after the Conquest, directed that "whosoever shall withhold this tenth part shall, by the justice of the bishop and the king, be forced to the payment of it, if need be." These provisions are part of the common law of England, and they effectually dispose of the idea that the tithe was a voluntary offering which the farmer to-day ought to pay because of the supposed piety of unknown ancestors.

The proceeds of the tithe—which originally, according to Blackstone, were " distributed in a fourfold division : one for the use of the bishop, one for maintaining the fabric of the church, a third for the poor, and a fourth to provide for the incumbent "—were the first great source of revenue to the Church ; but in the course of centuries that revenue was largely added to by gifts. It was not uncommon for a man to hand over his property to a monastery upon condition that he was allowed a sufficiency to keep him ; while the money given for the provision of masses for the dead was a considerable aid to the Church in the Middle Ages. And as the monks were exceedingly keen traders, their wealth was increased by farming, buying, and selling to a degree that at length tempted the cupidity of a rapacious king. It was during that period that our great cathedrals and all our old parish churches were built ; and when, because of a divorce dispute, the Eighth Henry resolved to cut the Church in England altogether adrift from the Church of Rome, he adopted a measure of Disendowment which, though not complete. was very sweeping, and proved in the most absolute form the right of the State to deal as it willed with the property of the Church.

In the preamble of the Act dissolving the lesser monasteries, it is declared that "the Lords and Commons, by a great deliberation, finally be resolved that it is and shall be much more to the pleasure of Almighty God, and for the honour of this His realm, that the possessions of such small religious houses, now being spent, spoiled, and wasted for increase and maintenance of sin, should be used and committed to better uses.' The State in this asserted a right it had never forfeited, and which, by successive Acts of Parliament, has been specifically retained. No one to-day would defend the fashion in which Henry took property which had been devoted to certain public uses and lavished it upon favourites and friends. The main point, however, is not the manner of disposal, but the fact that it could be disposed of at all ; and when any one doubts the power of the State regarding the property of the Church, a reference to what Parliament has done in the matter is sufficient to show constitutional precedent for Disendowment.

But though much was taken from the Church at the Reformation period, much was left, and it was left to a body differing in many important particulars from that which had been despoiled. As Mr. Arthur Elliott, M.P., a Whig writer, observes in his book " The State and the Church," " It would be to give a very false notion of the position of the Church towards the State to omit all mention of the sources from which, as regards its edifices, the Church of England finds itself so magnificently endowed. In the main, the wealth of the Church in this respect was inherited, or rather acquired, at the time of the Reformation, from the Roman Catholics, who had created it. The Roman Catholics and the English nation had been formerly one and the same. When the nation, for the most part, ceased to be Catholic, these edifices, like other endowments devoted to the religious instruction of the people, became the property of the Protestant Church of England, as by law established."

The new Act of Parliament Church—for it had its doctrines and its discipline defined by statute—became possessed, therefore, of the cathedrals, the churches, much of the glebe, and a large portion of the tithe that had been given or granted to the Roman Catholic communion, which had held the ground for centuries. And succeeding monarchs, with the exception of Mary, so confirmed and added to these gifts that "the Judicious Hooker" was led to exclaim—" It might deservedly be at this day the joyful song of innumerable multitudes, and (which must be eternally confessed, even with tears of thankfulness) the true inscription, style, or title of all churches as yet standing within this realm, ' By the goodness of Almighty God and His servant Elizabeth, we are.'"

And it was not only " His servant Elizabeth " who, among monarchs since the Reformation, has assisted the Houses of the Legislature to pecuniarily aid the Church. Queen Anne surrendered the first fruits, or profits of one year, of all spiritual promotions, and the tithe of the revenue of all sees, in order to create a fund for increasing the incomes of the poor clergy ; but Queen Anne's Bounty comes straight out of the national pocket, for, had our monarchs retained this source of income, it would have been taken into account when the Civil List was settled at the commencement of the reign, and at least £100,000 a year saved to the Exchequer. And the nation has even more directly helped the fund, Parliament having, between 1809 and 1829, voted considerably over a million towards it.

But this is not all. Dealing merely with national money appropriated to Church purposes during the present century, it may be added that in 1818 Parliament voted a million sterling for the purpose of building churches, that in 1824 a further sum of half a million was granted for the same purpose, and that a subsequent amount of close upon ninety thousand pounds has to be added to the total. And not only by large grants did Parliament help the Church. In the old days of Protection, when almost every conceivable article was taxed, the duty chargeable on the materials used in the building of churches was remitted, this amounting between 1817 and 1845 to over £336,000. A drawback was also granted on the paper used in printing the Prayer Book, and this, while the paper duty was levied, could scarcely have averaged less than a thousand a year. In small things, as in great, Parliament helped the Church, for an Act of George IV. specifically exempted from toll the carriage and horses used by a clergyman when driving to visit a sick parishioner.

I claim, therefore, that the State has a right to dispose of such property of the Church as was not given to it in recent times by private donors, knowing it would be appropriated to the purposes of a sect ; and I claim it because the tithes were law-created, because the bulk of the possessions passed from one communion to another by force of law, and because the State has continued to pecuniarily aid the Church throughout the centuries during which she has existed. And, if constitutional precedent be demanded, they are to be found in abundance upon the statute book, notably in the measures affecting the monasteries, the Tithe Commutation Act, and the Act putting an end to the Established Church in Ireland.

If it be urged, as it sometimes is, that, because the original royal ordinance enforcing tithes was granted before our regular parliamentary system was in existence, Parliament has no power to deal with it, it must be answered that in all matters within these realms, touching either life or property, Parliament is supreme. And, as bearing even more directly upon the point raised, it may be added that rights of toll and market, granted to boroughs by royal charter before Parliaments were chosen as at present, have been altered and abolished by Parliaments since ; and that Magna Charta itself, signed many years before Simon de Montfort called the first House of Commons into being, has been modified, and often modified, since that event.

If further proof be wanted, not only of the power but of the will of Parliament to interfere directly in the monetary affairs of an Established Church, the Act disendowing the Irish Establishment eighteen years ago, and another passed fifty years since, chopping and changing the salaries of the English bishops, may be referred to. And, regarding a further measure of the last half-century, the words of such a sturdy Conservative as Lord Brabourne, used in a letter written in 1887, are eminently satisfactory :—"The Tithe Commutation Act was nothing more nor less than the assertion by the State of its right to deal with tithes as national property."

But, it may be said, the property, whether contributed by private benefaction or royal grant, was distinctly given to the Church, and ought not, therefore, to be taken away. I dispute both points of the contention. The property was allotted to a Church which acknowledged the supremacy of the Pope, and it is used by one which abjures it ; to a Church possessed of seven sacraments, and used by one with only two ; to a Church believing in transubstantiation, and used by one holding that doctrine to be a dangerous heresy ; to a Church with an unmarried clergy, and used by one in which the large families of the poorer parsons are their stumbling-block and reproach ; to a Church which performed its most sacred mysteries in the Latin tongue, and used by one whose ceremonies are delivered in a language understanded of the people. If it be true that the Church to-day is the Church as it has always been, why, in the name of common reason, was Cranmer, the Protestant, burned by Mary, and Campion, the Jesuit, hanged by Elizabeth?

From the fact that the Church of England is not a corporation —that is, it has not property in its own right, and what is possessed by its members is vested in them not as proprietors but as trustees—there flows the consequence that it is mainly the life interests of those engaged in clerical work which have to be considered. And those life interests will be considered and generously dealt with when the time for disendowment arrives.

And then comes a question which many will deem of all-importance—"How is the Church to exist afterwards ?" or, to

put the point in the extremest fashion, and in the words
addressed to the clergy in the very first of the "Tracts for
the Times," "Should the Government of the country so far
forget their God as to cut off the Church, to deprive it of its
temporal honours and substance, on what will you rest the
claims to respect and attention which you make upon your
flock?" And the answer is that, if the Church be worthy to
exist, it will be able, like other religious bodies, to stand upon
the open and constant manifestation of its own excellences.

Look around and see what the voluntary system has done.
In England it has planted a place of worship in every corner of
the kingdom ; in Wales it has saved from spiritual starvation a
populace neglected by the Establishment ; in Scotland it has
founded a Free Church by sacrifices which were the marvel and
the pride of a preceding generation ; and in Ireland it has
secured to the mass of the people the ministrations of their own
religion, despite every bribe, persecution, and lure. Is it in
England, where the Episcopalian system has most that is
wealthy and all that is socially influential on its side, that a
State endowment is needed to provide for its professors what
the miners of Cornwall and the labourers of Carmarthen, the
hardy toilers in the Highlands, and the poverty-stricken
peasants of Connemara provide for themselves? If this be so,
then no greater indictment could be levelled against the process
of Establishment, no more certain proof could be afforded of
the evils which follow in its train, than that it produced such a
mean coldness of soul. But the supposition is so dishonouring
to the great body of church-goers that its use proves the straits
in which the defenders of the existing system find themselves.

Disendowment would undoubtedly reduce the larger salaries
allotted to the clergy, and probably increase the smaller. A
parson would then be paid according to his value to the parish,
whether as preacher or administrator, and he would not draw a
thousand a year for doing nothing, while his curate received
eighty or a hundred for performing the work. The Church
would no longer be a rich man's preserve, wherein younger
sons could obtain comfortable family livings, while their duty
was done by ill-paid deputies. We should no longer see an

Archbishop of Canterbury, with a salary of £15,000 a year, begging upon a public platform for worn-out garments for the poorer working clergy. A primate is conceivable at a third the cost, and the money thus saved to the Church alone would prevent the necessity for such a humiliating proceeding as openly asking for old clothes for toiling clergymen. With disendowment, in short, men would be paid according to their merits and not their family connections—according to their work and not their birth. And, further, the scandal of the sale of livings—the shame of the public advertisement of cures of souls as eligible according as they are in a hunting country, or near a fishing river, or close to "good society"—would be done away with. Would all these gains count as nothing to the Church, considered as a religious body?

The process of disendowment, then, is the necessary accompaniment of disestablishment; it is possible; it is just; and its effects would make for good. It is necessary, because if the Church is to be severed from the State on the ground that it has failed in its mission, it would be obviously out of the question to leave it possessed of the property given to it to secure that mission's due performance. It is possible, because Parliament is not merely supreme in all such matters, but has shown within the past few years its capacity for disendowing a Church having precisely the same rights and privileges as the English Establishment. It is just, because no one sect has the right to property granted it on the ground that it represented the religious sentiment of the whole nation. And it would make for good in giving a more distinctively religious character to the clergy, in paying them according to their deserts and not according to the length of the purse that purchased them their livings, and in freeing a religious system from the ignoble associations of the auction mart.

Upon these grounds it is demanded that, with disestablishment, disendowment shall come. Life interests will be respected; all modern gifts to the Episcopalians as a distinct sect will be fairly dealt with; further than this the Establishment is not entitled to demand, and further than this Liberals will not be prepared to go.

# XVI.—OUGHT EDUCATION TO BE FREE?

A QUESTION which is intimately connected in many minds with the Church is that of national education. It stood next to it in order in that early programme of Mr. Chamberlain which demanded " Free Church, free schools, free land, and free labour."

This matter of free schools is not likely to create as much opposition as it would have done even a short time since, for no question awaiting settlement is ripening so rapidly. Experience is teaching in an ever-increasing ratio that certain defects exist in our system of national education which hinder its full development, some of which, at least, could be avoided by the abolition of fees.

The progress which has been made in public opinion within only half a century regarding the amount of aid that should be given to elementary schools, encourages the hope that more will yet be given, and that very speedily. It is but a little more than fifty years ago that a Liberal Ministry led the way in devoting a portion of the national funds to this purpose; and no one unacquainted with the history of that period could guess the number and the weight of the obstacles thrown in the way of even such a modest proposal as that Ministry made. The Tories, while not particularly anxious that the mass of the people should be educated at all, were decidedly desirous that such teaching as was given should be under the direct control of the Church. Archbishops and bishops, Tories, high and low, joined to continually hamper the development of any system of national education which afforded the Nonconformists the least privilege; but despite their every effort the movement spread. The annual grant of £20,000, which was commenced in 1834, grew by leaps and bounds. In a little more than twenty years it had become nearly half a million for Great Britain alone ; in thirty years it had increased by close upon another quarter of a million ; and in fifty years (and the growth in the meantime had been mainly the fruit of the Education Act, passed by the Liberal Ministry in 1870) it had touched three millions. And that sum, vast as it was, represented only the amount granted from the national exchequer, being supplemented by an even larger total raised by local rates.

So far has the nation gone in the path of State-aided and rate-aided education, and the question is whether it is not worth while to go the comparatively little way further which is needed to make elementary education free. For the fees which are now paid do not represent a quarter of the amount which the teaching costs. And not only so, but the existence of these fees is a continual hindrance to the working of the Act. The effect of the fee is to keep out of the board schools thousands of children who ought to be in them ; and the attempt to enforce its payment increases the odium which almost necessarily attends upon compulsion.

" But," it will be said, " where a parent is too poor to pay, the fee can be remitted." That is true, and the extent to which the system of such remission is carried in some districts is one of the strongest arguments in favour of free education. It is desirable to get the children into the schools, but it is highly undesirable to do this by practically pauperizing the parents. If elementary education were free to all, all could partake of it without any appearance of favour on the one hand or shame on the other. But the independent poor have now the choice of making themselves still poorer by paying the fee for the education they are bound to have administered, or of losing their independence by asking the school board or the poor-law guardians for relief. And the consequence, of course, is that many who have no independence to lose, and are the least deserving of help, receive the assistance they are never backward to ask.

"What is worth having is worth paying for" is a remark sometimes made in this connection, but is it not as applicable to the State as to the individual? For it is for no philanthropic but for a decidedly practical reason that the country assists education. All men in these days admit that the most cultivated people, like the most cultivated individual man, has the best chance of success. With educated Germany, and educated France, and educated America pressing us hard, it is a necessity of existence for England to be equally educated. And seeing that the school board rate and the Government grant mount higher and higher and the fees become lower and lower, the only practical question is whether the State had not better boldly step in, abolish fees which are a hindrance to educational progress, pay the whole amount instead of three-quarters, and provide free teaching for all.

If such a consummation were secured, the status of what are now called voluntary schools would of necessity be materially altered. As at present applied, the name "voluntary" affixed to the schools of the National Society and similar bodies is very much a misnomer. It conveys that the schools are supported by voluntary subscriptions; but this is true in only a limited degree, for it is the Government grant—that is, money taken out of the pocket of every one who pays taxes, direct or indirect—which keeps them in existence. And, therefore, when Churchmen complain, as some of them are occasionally ill-advised enough to do, that they not only subscribe to their own schools but have to pay the rate as well, ought it not to be enough to remind them that their schools are supported not alone for educational but for sectarian purposes, and that, if they wish to proselytize, they must pay, in however inadequate a degree, for the privilege? The real hardship is that those who do not believe in the clerical system of education have to pay heavily by means of taxation to keep up establishments over which they have not the least control, and which are used by the clergy for denominational ends.

One result, then, of free education would be, not to destroy the voluntary schools, but to put them under the control of those who really and not nominally pay for keeping them up.

If Churchmen demand schools of their own, they must support them out of their own pocket and not out of other people's, though it may be well that, under a stringent "conscience clause" and with direct popular control, they should still share in the taxpayers' grants. As matters stand, the national schoolmaster is too often treated as if he were a mere servant of the clergyman, an idea which, with free education and popular government of all State-aided schools, would be bound to cease.

The cry raised by some clergymen when the Education Act was passed, that the undenominational system would be fruitful only in producing "astute scoundrels and clever devils," has died away. It is doubtful whether anybody ever really believed it; it is certain that no man with a reputation to lose would now repeat it. And, that being the case, the excuse for keeping up at the public expense two rival sets of schools—one sectarian and the other undenominational—has so largely disappeared that the onus of proving its necessity lies upon its advocates, and the burden of paying for it should be shifted upon the right shoulders.

Of course it is said that this proposal of free education is only another step towards Socialism, but no one should be frightened by phrases. Socialism has as many varieties as religion—some as bad and some as good—and from them must be selected those worth having. If, upon consideration of the whole case, free education be thought to be one of these, the fact that it is called Socialistic will not weigh to its disadvantage with a single sensible man.

What, then, is it that is asked, and why is it demanded? It is asked that elementary schools shall be freed from fees, and entirely supported out of the public funds, local and imperial; that advanced and technical education shall be made cheap and accessible, in order that those who want to progress can do so with as few hindrances as possible; and that all schools supported by public money shall be placed under popular control, and the schoolrooms, out of educational hours, made available for public use.

These things are demanded because by the present arrangements the progress of compulsion is hampered, the deserving and independent poor are inequitably dealt with, and the cost of collecting the fees is out of all proportion to their value when received. Already the public pay three-quarters of the cost of elementary education, and they do it for the benefit of the community ; if payment of the remaining quarter would increase the efficiency of the system, even only to a corresponding degree, it would be worth making. "Vested interests" might object ; but the national welfare must override them, though there is no intention of dealing with them otherwise than fairly. Due allowance would be made for the subscriptions which have been raised towards the erection and support of the voluntary schools ; but the nation has rights as well as individuals, and, in considering any compensation which may be demanded by the managers of such institutions, if free education be adopted, the public money which has been expended upon them must be taken into account equally with the private.

This much is certain : although England will not be able to hold her own simply with "the three R's," and advanced and technical education should, therefore, be widely spread, it is our duty to make "the three R's" as widely known as we can. It is not a question of principle, but of policy. Opposition to any education at all for the masses has disappeared ; the State and the parish already pay most of the cost ; if the system can be made more perfect by the abolition of fees, fees will have to be abolished.

# XVII.—DO THE LAND LAWS NEED REFORM?

IMMEDIATELY the question of the land is touched, a whole host of opponents to progress are roused to fierce and continuous action, though, as all politicians in these days affect a belief in the necessity for land reform, the question appears at first to be more one of degree than of principle. But, at the very outset, it is necessary to face the fact that there is an active propaganda going on which denies that any reform, even the most sweeping, will be of avail, and asserts that it is the very existence of private property in land which must be done away with.

In what is termed " Land Nationalization " a very dangerous fallacy exists. The first thing to be asked of any one who advocates it is to define the term. It is vague ; it is high-sounding ; but what does it mean ? If it means that the State is to take into its keeping all the land without compensating the present holders, it proposes robbery ; if it means that the process is to be accompanied by compensation, it would entail jobbery. There are thousands who, by working hard, have saved sufficient to buy a small plot on which to erect a house. Is that plot to be seized by the State without payment ? And if fair payment be given, and the taint of theft thus removed, does a single soul imagine that a Government department would be able to manage the land better than it is managed at present? Are our Government departments such models of efficiency and economy that such a belief can be entertained for a moment? What may fairly be demanded of all advocates of the nationalization or municipalization of the land is that they shall clearly show that the process would be honest in itself, just to the present holders, and likely to benefit the whole community. Unless they can do all these things, generalities are of no avail.

The land, it is sometimes urged, has been stolen from the people; but it cannot have been stolen from those who never directly possessed it : and, whatever may be said of the manner in which the large properties were secured centuries ago, much of the land has changed hands so often that most, at least, of the present holders have fairly paid for it. There is an old legal doctrine that the title of that which is bought in open market cannot afterwards be called in question, and that applies to the present case. And when we are told that there cannot exist private property in land because that commodity is a gift of God to all, is it not the fact that, in an old country like ours, land is worth little except it be highly cultivated ; that the labour, the manure, and the seed are private property without the shadow of a doubt ; and that it is these we largely have to pay for when agricultural commodities are bought ? Upon the same ground it is sometimes contended that we should have our water free because it falls from the heavens ; but nature did not provide reservoirs, or lay mains, or bring the pipes into our houses ; and for the sake of obtaining water easily we must pay for the labour and appliances used in collecting and distributing it. And the value of these illustrations, both as to land and to water, is to teach an avoidance of sounding generalities and a resolve to look at all questions in a practical light.

Recognizing, therefore, that private property in land has existed, is existing, and is not likely to be abolished, the duty of progressive politicians is to see how the laws affecting it can be so modified as to benefit a considerably larger portion of the community than at present. And three of the points which have been most discussed, and which now are nearest settlement, are the custom of primogeniture, the law of entail, and the enactments relating to transfer.

After spurning for many years the Liberal demand for the abolition of the custom of primogeniture—by which the land of a man dying without a will passes to the eldest son, to the exclusion of the rest of the family—the Tories in 1887 themselves proposed it ; and in the House of Lords only one peer had sufficient courage to stand up in defence of a custom which the whole peerage had sworn by until that time. It puzzles any one not a peer to understand how a distinctly dishonest practice could have existed so long, save for the utterly inade- quate reason that its tendency was to prevent large estates from being broken up, and that there were those who imagined that large estates were a benefit to the country. In actual working, however, it did not affect the largest estates but the smallest, and primogeniture was thus a question touching much more closely those of moderate means than the possessors of great wealth. A large holder of land is an exceedingly unlikely person to die without a will ; a small holder frequently does so, with the result of much injustice to and suffering among his family.

A practical instance is worth a hundred theories upon a point like this, and here are some such which have come under my own notice within the past few months. A man possessed of a small landed property died intestate ; his daughter, who had ministered to his wants for years, was left penniless, the whole of the property going to the eldest son. Another similarly circumstanced, whose stay and comfort during his old age had likewise been a daughter, shrank, with the foolish obstinacy of the superstitious, from making a will ; his friends, recognizing that, if he failed in this obvious duty, the daughter would be thrown without a penny on the world, while the eldest son, who for various reasons had not the least claim upon his father, would take everything, besought the old man to act reasonably ; and almost at the last moment he did. In a third case, a fisher- man, who for eighteen years had been paying for a piece of land through a building society, was drowned in a squall ; and his savings, designed for the support of himself and his wife, were swept straight into the pocket of his eldest son. Now in all these instances, had the money been invested in houses, ships, consols—in fact, anything but land—it would, in case of no will being made, have been divided among the whole family in fair proportion. The accident of it being put into land caused wrong and suffering in two cases, and wrong and suffering were very narrowly avoided in the third. The abolition of primogeniture, therefore, is much more needed by the working and the middle classes than by the rich, whose lawyers very seldom allow them to die without a will.

The law of entail is on its last legs, as well as the custom of primogeniture, and the Tories, by Lord Cairns' Settled Land Act, and a subsequent amending measure, have practically admitted that it is doomed. Entail affects the community by giving power to a man to fetter his land with a multitude of restrictions for an indefinite period ; it makes the nominal owner only in reality a life tenant ; and by cramping him upon the one side with conditions which may have become out of date, and tempting him on the other to limit his expenditure on that which is not wholly his own, the development of the land is impeded, and the progress of agriculture hampered by force of law. Entail, like primogeniture, has been defended on the ground that it tends to keep large estates intact ; but it is now so generally believed that a more widespread diffusion of land is desirable, that it is only necessary here to state the argument.

A more widespread diffusion of the land will not, however, be attained unless the process of transfer is at once cheapened and simplified. The lawyers reap too much advantage from the present system, and many a man refrains from buying a plot he would like because the cost of transfer unduly raises the price. If it were provided that all estates should be registered and their boundaries clearly defined, there would be no more difficulty and expense in transferring a piece of land than is now involved in selling a ship. In these days buyer and seller are parted by parchments ; and many who would like a plot, but who do not see why they should pay, because of the lawyers, ten, or fifteen, or twenty per cent. more than its value, put their money into concerns in which meddlesomeness created by Act of Parliament does not mingle.

Simpler and cheaper transfer would be a step towards the more general ownership of land by those who till it. Let all artificial aids to the holding together large estates by power of Parliament be abolished, let transfer be cheapened and simplified, and then let him who likes buy. Free trade in land is what we ask, and when it is attained land will be able to be dealt with the same as any other commodity, and those who want a piece can have it by paying for it.

But although it may not be desirable for the State to interfere in England for the creation of a peasant proprietary, it is needful that Parliament should do something tangible in the direction of securing allotments for the labourers. Upon that point, as upon primogeniture and entail, the Tories profess to be converted ; but as their Allotments Bill of 1887 appears in practice to be a sham, it is necessary that such amendments should be introduced as may render it a reality.

# XVIII.—SHOULD WASTE LANDS BE TILLED AND THE GAME LAWS ABOLISHED?

A DOZEN or fourteen years ago the questions attempted now to be answered were put much more frequently than at present. In the last days of the first Gladstone Administration and the earliest of the second Government of Mr. Disraeli, Liberals were looking for other worlds to conquer ; and many of them, not venturing upon such bold courses on the land question as have since been adopted by even moderate politicians, fastened their attention upon the waste lands and the game laws. No great results came from the movement ; other and more striking questions forced themselves to the front ; and we are almost as far from a legislative settlement of the two just mentioned as in the days of a more restricted suffrage.

This is the more surprising because the points named are of practical importance to the agricultural labourer, and the agricultural labourer now holds the balance of political power. But it is not likely that this state of quietude upon two such burning topics will long continue, for the country voter is certain soon to profit by the example of his brethren in the towns, and to demand that his representatives shall attend to those concerns immediately affecting his interests.

And first as to the question of waste lands. Town-bred theorists who have never walked over a mile of moorland are apt sometimes to talk as if all the uncultivated land in the country was in that condition because of the wicked will of those who own it, and to argue that, if only an Act of Parliament

could be secured, the waste lands would blossom like the rose.
They have the same touching faith in the efficacy of legislation
as had Lord Palmerston when he put aside some difficulty with
the exclamation, " Give me an Act of Parliament, and the thing
will be done." But facts are often too strong for legislation,
however well intentioned and skilfully devised, and those about
much of our waste land come within the list.

A large portion of uncultivated land is mountain and moor,
the greater part of which it would be impossible to make pro-
ductive at any price, and the remainder could not be turned to
account under a sum which would never make a profitable return. Those who think it an easy matter to cultivate waste land
should visit that portion of Dartmoor which is dominated by ·
the convict establishment. There they would see many an acre
reclaimed, but, if they were told the cost in money and labour,
they would be convinced that, were it not for penal purposes,
both money and labour might be put to better use elsewhere.
And if it be argued that the State should step in and advance
all that is required to cultivate such waste as can by any possibility be brought under the plough, it must be asked why the
taxpayer (for in this connection the State and the taxpayer are
one and the same) should add to his burdens for so small a
return.

But there is, without doubt, a large amount of land in this
country which now produces nothing, and which could be made
to produce a deal. That which is absorbed by huge private
parks, scattered up and down the kingdom, forms a great portion of this ; and though, for reasons which are mainly sentimental, one would not wish to see all such private parks turned
into sheep-walks or turnip-fields, there is the consideration that
property—and peculiarly property in land—has its duties as well
as its rights, and that those who wish to derive pleasure from
the contemplation of large spaces of cultivable but not cultivated
land, and in this way prevent such from being of any direct
value to the community, ought to pay for the privilege. The
rating of property of this kind at the present moment is ridiculously low ; it should at least be made as high as if the land
were devoted to some distinctly useful end.

As with parks, so with sporting lands. The rating of the latter is utterly inadequate ; and although it may be true that much of the land, especially in England, devoted to sporting purposes, is of little value for anything else, it is equally true that a great deal of it, particularly in Scotland, is fit for cultivation, and that tenants have been cleared from it to make room for deer and grouse. In all cases where the land would have value if culti- vated, the owner ought to be made pay as if that value were obtained, seeing that for his own pleasure he is depriving the community of the chance of obtaining increased food. It would be too drastic a measure to adopt the Chinese method of hanging proprietors who did not till cultivable land ; but many a land- owner, if made to feel his duty through his pocket, would do that duty rather than pay.

From the question of sporting lands to that of the game laws is a very short step. It may be that we have heard less of the latter during the last few years, because the Hares and Rabbits Act, passed by the second Gladstone Government in the first flush of its power, has done much to reconcile the tenant-farmers to the present state of things, by removing the grievance they most keenly felt.

The Act referred to provides (to quote Mr. Sydney Buxton's summary) " that every occupier of land shall have an inalienable right to kill the ground game (hares and rabbits) concurrently with any other person who may be entitled to kill it on the same land ; that the ground game may only be killed by the occupier himself or by persons duly authorized by him in writing ; that the use of firearms is confined to himself and one other, and they may only be used during the day ; that those authorized to kill the game in other ways (poison and traps, except in rabbit-holes, are prohibited) must be resident members of his household, persons in his ordinary service, and any one other person whom he employs for reward to kill the game ; that tenants on lease do not come under the provisions of the Act until the termination of their lease."

This was such a concession to the tenant-farmers that it is little wonder that those of them who had groaned under the ground game should have felt generally satisfied with it ; and although a wail has been going up from certain sportsmen that if the Act be not speedily amended the hare will become as extinct as the mastodon, it is not the least likely to be altered in the direction they wish. If amended at all, it will be so as to bring winged game within its provisions.

No one acquainted with rural life can doubt that the game laws, as at present administered, are a fruitful source of demoralization and crime. They demoralize all round, for they pollute the seat of justice by allowing such game preservers as are county magistrates to wreak vengeance upon all who transgress upon their pleasures ; they lower the moral standard of the gamekeepers, whose miserable employment turns them into spies of a peculiarly unpleasing description ; they make the rural police a standing army for the preservation of game ; and they consign to gaol many a man who, but for these laws, would be honest and free.

Such as would see justice most openly travestied should sit in a country police court and hear game cases tried. Let them notice the ostentatious fashion in which some magistrate, while a summons in which his game is concerned is being heard, will (as is carefully noted in the local papers) " withdraw from the bench " by taking his chair a foot back from his fellows and friends. Let them hear evidence upon which no man charged with any other offence would ever be convicted. Let them see the vindictive sentences that are passed. And then let them go home and think over the fashion in which that which is nicknamed "justice " is administered to any man unlucky enough to have offended a gamekeeper or a policeman, and to be charged as a poacher.

In the good old hanging days, a man was sentenced to death in a western county for sheep-stealing. The sentence was the usual one, but other sheep-stealers had been let off the capital penalty for so many years that it was greatly to the astonishment of the district that this one was hanged. Then people began to think, and, remembering that he had the reputation of being a clever poacher, they saw that he had been paid off for the new and the old. It is much the same in the rural districts to-day. In game cases the presumption of the English

law courts that a man shall be held to be innocent until he is
proved guilty is systematically reversed. The unsupported
word of a gamekeeper is considered to be worth that of half-a-
dozen ordinary men ; and it is not uncommon for a defendant
convicted of some offence, totally unconnected with the game
laws, to have his penalty increased because the superintendent
of police has whispered to the justices' clerk, and the clerk to
the magistrates, the fatal word "poacher." Those who live in a
town can scarcely conceive the open fashion in which justice is
degraded by the county magistrates when the game is in question. But, if any would bring it home to themselves—and the
strongest words are too faint to picture the reality—let them go
to some rural court, where the justices do not imagine that the
light of public opinion can be brought to bear upon them, and
see how poachers are tried.

If it were only because of the widespread demoralization they
cause, the game laws ought to be repealed. They are avowedly
kept up for the benefit of the class which does little or no work,
and they fill the prisons at our expense to preserve a sport in
which we have no share and no wish to share. And, if they are
to be retained on the statute book at all, their administration
should, at the very least, be taken from those who are practically
prosecutor, jury, and judge in one, and placed in impartial
hands.

# XIX.—OUGHT LEASEHOLDS TO BE EN-FRANCHISED?

THE proposal to enfranchise leaseholds—that is, to enable a leaseholder, upon paying a fair price, to claim that his tenure be turned into freehold—is a comparatively new one in the field of practical politics ; but it has come to the front so rapidly that it is already far nearer solution than others which have agitated the public mind for many years. The grievance had for a long time been felt, and in some parts of the kingdom sorely felt ; but a ready remedy had not suggested itself, and the subject slept.

The grievance is this—that the present system of leases for lives or for a term of years causes frequent loss to the lease-holder and much injury to the community, benefiting only the owner of the soil. The remedy would be to empower a lease-holder to demand from the ground landlord that the land shall be transferred to him upon payment of its fair value, as appraised by some public tribunal.

And first as to the results which flow from the present state of things. These vary with the circumstances, and some of the circumstances demand study. Leases, broadly speaking, are of two kinds—those which are granted on lives and those which are for a specified term of years. Of the two, the former are the more objectionable, as they frequently work gross injustice. A lease is granted which shall expire at the death of the third of three persons named in the deed. Under that lease a man builds a house ; the first life expires, and the leaseholder has to pay a fine—or, as it is called, a heriot—of a specified sum ; the second dies, and another fine has to be paid ; and when the third passes away, the property and all upon it revert to the landlord. Is it not easy to see that no particular chapter of accidents is required to terminate any three given lives within a comparatively short period, while, if an epidemic occurred, ground landlords everywhere would reap a rich harvest from the ready falling in of leases for lives?

One instance out of thousands may be quoted of how the system works. " A piece of land which let for £2 an acre as an agricultural rent was let for building purposes at £9 an acre, and divided into eleven plots. On one of these a poor man built a cottage, at a cost of £60, on a ground rent of 16s. 6d. The term was for three lives and one in reversion. The charge for the lease was £5. On the expiration of each of the three lives £1 was payable as a fine or heriot, and £10 was to be paid on nominating the life in reversion. All the four lives expired in twenty-eight years. The landlord thereupon took possession of the house. He had thus received in twenty-eight years, besides the annual ground rent, the following sums :—£5 for the lease, £10 for nomination of life in reversion, £3 as heriot on the expiration of the three lives—in all £18 ; and, in addition, the house built at the expense of the victim, which he sold for £58."

The reply may be made, " But, granting that leases for lives often have cruel results, is not the remedy in the hands of those who want leases ? Why do they take those for lives?" For this reason—that in some parts of the country it is the only way by which a building plot can be obtained, and that, as long as the possibility of securing so good a bargain is legalized, so long will the more unscrupulous among the landlords force an intending tenant to accept that or nothing.

Leases for long terms of years do not as readily lend themselves to the chance of legal robbery, but they have their own ill effects. Houses are built in flimsy fashion upon the express idea that they are intended to last only the specified term ; and during the expiring years of the lease, repairs are grudged, and the dwellings rendered unhealthy to the occupier and unsafe to the passers-by. If a man has a house which is erected upon

8

leasehold land, and therein builds up, by his own skill and industry, a good business, he is absolutely at the mercy of the ground landlord when the lease expires. The rent is raised because of the success his own faculties have secured, onerous conditions in the way of repairs are imposed, and what can he do? "If you don't like it, you can leave it," is the landlord's reply ; but there is many a business which does not bear transplanting, and if the tenant be on a large estate it might happen that, if he did not accede to the owner's terms, he would have to move to a far-distant part of the town, or even—as at Devonport and Huddersfield among other places—out of the town altogether, and that would mean ruin. And thus he is practically compelled to struggle on in order to increase the wealth of the landlord, who has done nothing, at the expense of himself, who has done all.

And this is not always the worst, for in many cases landlords for various reasons will not renew at any price, and the tenant has perforce to go the moment his lease expires. A certain Whig duke—and, of course, a zealous defender of "the rights of property"—conceived the idea, upon coming into his estates some years ago, that a village stood too near his park gates. Not brooking that herdsmen and traders should stand between the wind and his nobility, he directed that, as leases fell in, the tenants should be cleared out, graciously, however, offering them other plots some three miles away. And the tenants had to leave the homes in which they had been born and where their parents had lived before them, and to see them tumble down in utter ruin, in order that so mighty a person as a duke should not be shocked by the sight of the common herd. It was one of the thousand cases in life where a man had a right to do that which it was not right for him to perform.

Another fashion in which grievous injustice to the leaseholder can be done is frequently illustrated. It has happened, and happened very recently, that a ground landlord has granted leases for a term of years ; that, upon the strength of these agreements, houses have been built ; and that upon the landlord's decease it has been discovered by some skilful lawyer that the dead man had had no power, under an entail or settlement, to grant such leases ; whereupon the heir has invoked the law to cancel the whole, and has seized everything upon the land. This is legal, but is it commonly honest ?

In other ways the leasehold system is an injury not only to individuals but to the community. A west country town, where all the land is held by one man, has been crippled in every attempt to expand and improve by the impossibility of obtaining a freehold plot. What person in his senses would erect a substantial factory or a large concern of any kind upon a comparatively short lease? Men embark upon such enterprises in order that, as year follows year, their property may become more valuable, not that year by year it may become less so by the growing nearness of the time when it will pass to the landlord, who has never contributed a penny or a thought to the success of the concern, the building containing which, at the expiration of the lease, he can call his own.

For all these unfairnesses to individuals, hindrances to trade, and injuries to the community, is proposed the remedy stated— that a leaseholder who has twenty (or, as some suggest, ten or fifteen) years to run, shall be empowered to demand that his land be made freehold upon the payment of its value, as assessed by some specified tribunal.

The first objection is that this would be an undue interference with "the rights of property." But it has already been laid down by Parliament that such "rights" can be set aside in the public interest upon the payment of fair compensation ; and what has been done in regard to the making of railways can be done respecting the building or the preserving of houses. The existing system is an injury to the community ; and as the price to be paid for its abolition, whether wholly or in part, would be assessed by a tribunal constituted by Parliament, the landlords would have no more reason to complain than they now have when compelled to sell a portion of their property to a railway company.

The next plea is that it would interfere with "freedom of contract." Upon the general question of what that freedom is, how far it now exists, and in how large a degree the State has a right to interfere with it, one need not speak, for in this matter of leases Parliament has already stepped in to "interfere with freedom of contract." It having been found that some landlords were accustomed to insert in leases oppressive provisions for forfeiture in certain conditions, the Legislature empowered the courts to lift from the leaseholders covenants which unduly burdened them. And if a precedent is asked for the particular remedy proposed, the Acts enabling any copyholder to enfranchise his holding should be consulted.

If it be said that, should such a power be granted by law, no one possessing land would let on a long lease, it may be answered that this would be no great evil, seeing how the leasehold system has worked. But as landowners will want in the future as in the past to let or to sell, and as it is not to be supposed that any man will take a lease of less than twenty years and build upon the land, the owners will accommodate themselves to circumstances, and dispose of their property as best they can.

Owners in other countries do so, and why not here? Such a leasehold system as that of England is practically unknown elsewhere. In France, it is true, something of the kind exists, but we seek for it in vain in Germany and Austria, in Russia and Switzerland, or in Spain and Portugal; while in Italy, where no leases for over thirty years are permitted, a tenant can convert his property into freehold by redeeming the rent.

The supporters of leasehold enfranchisement, therefore, have on their side not only the practical evils of the present system, but parliamentary precedent and continental custom. These should suffice to persuade all who study the matter that the time for a change has come, and that the way in which that change is proposed to be effected is just and equitable.

# XX.—WHOSE SHOULD BE THE UN-EARNED INCREMENT?

THERE is a school of politicians which reply to all such pro-posals as have been sketched for practical land reform : " They do not go far enough, for they would merely transfer the un-earned increment from the present freeholders to the present leaseholders, and we want it transferred to the community." This "unearned increment" is a matter of which we are likely to hear a deal in the immediate future, for since John Mill stated the theory it has been much talked of, and to-day more than ever. It is sometimes contended, in fact, that, supposing all the projected reforms carried and in full and untrammeled action, "the absorption of the unearned increment by private individuals would perpetuate an evil which would swallow up whatever good those reforms might have a tendency to bring about."

What then is the theory upon which so much may depend? It cannot be better stated than in the words of Mill :—"Sup-pose that there is a kind of income which constantly tends to increase, without any exertion or sacrifice on the part of the owners : those owners constituting a class in the community, whom the natural course of things progressively enriches, con-sistently with complete passiveness on their own part. In such a case it would be no violation of the principles on which private property is grounded, if the State should appropriate this increase of wealth, or part of it, as it arises. This would not properly be taking anything from anybody ; it would merely be applying an accession of wealth, created by circumstances, to the benefit of society, instead of allowing it to become an unearned appendage to the riches of a particular class. Now this is actually the case with rent."

When Mill's " Principles of Political Economy" was published, this theory of the State absorbing, in whole or in part, the " unearned increment " of the land, was regarded by many as so utopian that it was put aside with a scoff, and was thought to have been settled with a sneer. But it has struck deep root into many a Radical mind, and those who believe in it ask it to be shown how it is either dishonest as a theory or would be impossible in practice.

There need be no attempt to do either, for Mill himself made an important restriction in his definition of what should be done which relieves it from the stigma of dishonesty or impracticability. He believed that " it would be no violation of the principles on which private property is grounded, if the State should appropriate this increase of wealth, *or part of it,* as it arises." It may be agreed that the State could fairly appropriate a part of this increment, and this might be done by means of taxation. But that is a very different matter from taking the whole.

One who argues in favour of the latter plan, submits this contention :—" The area of a county, for purposes of illustration, may be taken as a fixed quantity. Now, the demand for land will increase, and as a corollary the price of land will rise, exactly in proportion to the increase of population. This additional value is not brought about by either independent industry, ingenuity, or the outlay of capital on the part of any private individual : it is a growth entirely due to the increase of the community : it is of enormous value, is extracted from the dire necessities of the whole population, and goes into the pockets of private individuals who have never done anything to create it."

But does the illustration hold good whether applied to such a limited area as a county or to the country at large ? It is not the case that the demand for land increases and its price rises exactly in proportion to population ; and it is as little the case that its increased value, if any, is "extracted from the dire necessities of the whole population." For while the number of our inhabitants is increasing, the value of such land as ministers directly to their wants in the provision of food and clothing is decreasing. If all the bread that is eaten, beef that is killed, and wool that is worn, were raised within these shores, there would be a semblance of truth in the illustration ; but we have left the days when we lived on our own produce far behind, and the British farmer would only be too happy if the picture thus presented were even approximately like reality.

It may be replied that bread and beef and wool do not exhaust the catalogue of men's requirements from the land ; and they do not, for we require plots upon which to build, and good houses are just as necessary as cheap food. But even where land is made more valuable by its becoming used for building purposes, is there any justice in either the State or a municipality taking the whole increased value ? Let the case be that of a man who thinks that he sees a chance of a town expanding, and who purchases a piece of land which will be of little use to anybody unless his idea proves correct, but which will bring him a good profit if he has skilfully foreseen. Why should he not be as fairly paid for his skill and foresight as if he had bought a house on a similar belief ? The reply is, "The quantity of land is limited ; that of houses is not ;" but that is only true up to a certain and very definite point ; and with the reforms which have already been suggested, and with a fairer system of taxing the land, the community would gain all it could fairly ask.

My contention, shortly put, is this—That the State has a right to share in the increased value of all property, landed or otherwise ; and that, in the case of land, it has an additional, though limited, claim, because of the conditions upon which that commodity passed into private ownership. Those who work for wages have to pay income tax immediately those wages touch a certain point ; as they rise, so does the payment increase ; and, after a given amount, the tax is proportionately much heavier. Why should not the same principle be applied to income of every sort from land as to income of every sort from wages, profits, or invested capital ?

It is not so at present, as a study of the land tax will show. Nominally that tax is four shillings in the pound on the full annual value, but actually what does it stand at ? It was fixed by Parliament in the seventeenth century, the semi-owners of the land, who had held their property under certain weighty conditions of contributing military strength to the King, and who had managed by degrees to slip through their obligations, agreeing thus to tax themselves as a compensation for the burden that had been lifted from them. But in 1798 it was enacted—by a Parliament in which practically only landowners were represented—that the valuation upon which the tax was to be paid should be that of 1692, when on its then conditions it was first levied. And the consequence is that, although this later Act directed that it should be assessed and collected with impartiality, in parts of the country which have stood still the tax now is not far from the original sum, while it amounts in the immediate neighbourhood of such a city as Liverpool to about a fifth of a farthing in the pound. It may not be feasible, because of the manner in which much of the impost has been "redeemed," and it might in some cases be unjust, to raise the land tax at once to four shillings in the pound on the valuation of 1888 instead of 1692 ; but the same Parliament which put the clock back has the power to bring it up to the proper time ; and, at least, something could be done to lessen the loss the State is now made to suffer.

There is another way in which landowners could justly be called upon to pay a portion of the unearned increment to the State, and that is through the taxation of ground-rents. This is a point which keenly touches the towns, and deserves the early attention of Parliament. At present the great ground landlords escape their fair share of the burdens which fall heavily upon those who take their leases. And, so certain are some of them that the taxing time will soon come, that they are already selling a portion of their town estates, so as to " get out from under " before that period arrives.

It may therefore be submitted that, with a fairer land tax and the taxation of ground rents, we should secure to the State the proportion of the " unearned increment " to which she is justly entitled: Those who would go further must be prepared to prove that property in land is so different in every essential from all other kinds that it would be honest for the State to absorb the whole unearned increment of the one, and to levy only an income and property tax on the other.

# XXI.—HOW SHOULD LOCAL
## SELF-GOVERNMENT BE EXTENDED?

It is always consolatory to find amid the welter of party politics some topic upon which all say they agree, and such a topic certainly is that of the reform of local government. Politicians of every shade have long professed their desire for such a reform, and it ought now to be within measurable distance of accomplishment.

Upon the great question of the extension of self-government to Ireland I have already spoken ; and in regard to the purely domestic affairs of all the four divisions of the kingdom— England, Scotland, and Wales, as well as Ireland—it need only here be added that the solution of much of the difficulty which springs from an overburdened Parliament will be found in devolving upon a special authority for each the right of dealing with its own local concerns. But, as to three of the four divisions, it is not so pressing a question as that which is commonly known as the reform of local government, and the main proposition touching which is summed up in the demand for county councils.

This is a matter which more intimately touches the country districts than the towns, for in all the latter of any size there are popularly elected municipal councils, which exercise much power over local affairs. The only exception is the greatest town of all, for London was specifically exempted (by the action of the House of Lords) from the reform effected in all other cities and boroughs by the Municipal Corporations Act of 1835. There is a Corporation of the City of London ; but this body,

against which a very great deal can be said, has authority only
over one square mile of ground, the remaining 119 square miles
upon which the metropolis stands being governed by vestries,
. trustee boards, and district boards of works, all connected with
and subject to the Metropolitan Board of Works—or Board of
Words, as it was once irreverently but truly called—which is
not chosen directly by the ratepayers, but is selected by the
vestries, who themselves are elected by handfuls of people, the
general public paying them no heed. And thus it comes to pass
that the greatest and wealthiest city in the world is worse
governed than the smallest of our municipal boroughs, for nine
out of ten ratepayers take not the least interest in electing the
vestries, and not one ratepayer in a hundred could tell the name
of his district representative on the Metropolitan Board of
Works, now proposed, by even a Conservative Administration,
to be abolished.

It is not a small concern, this of reforming the government
of London, for it affects four millions of people—a number not
far short of the population of Ireland ; but politicians in the
mass, as even the keenest metropolitan municipal reformer will
admit, are more interested in the general question of local
government.

Speaking broadly, the defects of the system proposed to be
reformed are that of the popularly elected bodies there are too
many, and that the great governing body is not elected at all.
In a certain town of 3000 inhabitants, there are at this moment
a Town Council, a School Board, a Burial Board, and (because
under the Public Health Act an adjoining parish was tacked on)
a Local Board of Health ; while, notwithstanding that it sends
representatives to a Board of Guardians for the whole Union,
it had until recently, and in addition to the other bodies, a
Local Board of Guardians, chosen under a special Act. And,
beyond all these, a Highway Board meets within its borders,
which has to be consulted and negotiated with whenever a road
leading into the town needs to be re-metalled or an additional
brick is required for a neighbouring bridge.

As if all these boards were not sufficient to keep the district
in good order, there is the Court of Quarter Sessions, which has

jurisdiction in various details that the multitude of small bodies cannot touch. These latter have one justification, however, that the former cannot claim, and that is that, despite there being magistrates who are members of the boards of guardians by virtue of their office, and although the more property one possesses the more votes one can give for certain of the local bodies, these in the main are popularly elected, and are, therefore, directly responsible to the ratepayers for the manner in which their trust is used.

It is quite otherwise with the Court of Quarter Sessions. This consists only of magistrates, such magistrates being appointed by the Lords-Lieutenant of counties, and the appointments being made mainly on political grounds. As a rule, the holders of that distinguished position are Tories, and they take good care that the magistrates shall be Tories also. It is not long since it would have been impossible to find a single Liberal on the commission of the peace for Huntingdonshire ; and when comparatively recently it was pointed out to the Lord-Lieutenant of Essex that an almost exactly similar state of things prevailed in that shire, he replied he did not consider there was a Liberal in the whole county who was socially qualified for the magisterial bench. The idea of making a banker or a merchant a justice of the peace was too shocking ; and thus the commercial classes and a good half of the population (giving the other half to the Tories) were completely unrepresented, not merely on the bench, but in the Court of Quarter Sessions, which governed the affairs and spent the money of the county.

There is no necessity to prove that these courts have spent the county monies wantonly or with conscious impropriety in order to show this condition of things to be wrong. In imperial affairs, the doctrine that taxation without representation is tyranny has been asserted to the full ; in municipal matters, since the Act of 1835, the same has prevailed ; but in county concerns it has been non-existent. The magistrates represent no one but themselves, their party, and their own class; they are necessarily swayed by the passions and prejudices that party and class possess ; and, seeing that the English people long ago refused power over the national purse to an unrepresentative body like the House of Lords, it is surprising they have until now allowed power over the local purse to be in the hands of such equally unrepresentative bodies as the courts of quarter sessions.

The line which the immediate reform of local government must take is, therefore, the creation of a directly-elected body to deal with county affairs, and the federation of such of the smaller boards as have to do with the more purely district concerns, both of which points the Cabinet of Lord Salisbury appear disposed to concede. But upon the former point, Liberals will claim that the whole—and not merely three-fourths—of the County Councils shall be directly elected, for the system of aldermen, included in the Municipal Reform Act by the House of Lords, has been used for partisan purposes, as it was intended to be, and the same effect will follow in the case of the counties if the same cause is provided.

Any system, in fact, which involves " double election " tends to make the body concerned hidebound and cliquish. A county alderman once chosen, especially if he were a squire, as he most likely would be, would have to behave himself in most outrageous fashion ever to lose his post. The ratepayers might grumble, but it would be difficult in the extreme to dislodge him, for he would be removed from their direct control, and the Council would consider it ungracious to get rid of an '' old servant." If one wants to know how this double election operates, let him ask some clear-sighted Londoner who is acquainted with the manner in which his own city is ruled. He will be answered that for scandalous and wanton expenditure not many bodies can equal the Metropolitan Asylums Board, the members of which are mainly chosen by the various boards of guardians ; while for jobbery and general mismanagement it is even beaten by the Metropolitan Board of Works, which is elected by the several vestries. And he will add that this chiefly arises from the fact that the ratepayers have no direct control over either of these bodies, and that the good result of such direct control was shown by this fact—that when the metropolitan ratepayers considered that the School Board, which is directly elected, was practising extravagance, they placed at the bottom of the poll those responsible for the policy, with the effect that considerable savings were speedily effected.

And therefore now, when County Councils are being established, all Liberals will have very carefully to watch the points upon which the Tories and Whigs may combine in an attempt to give the country a semblance without the reality of representative local self-government. What must be insisted upon is—(1) That the Councils shall be entirely elective ; (2) that the ratepayers shall directly elect ; (3) that there shall be no property qualification for membership ; (4) that the voting shall be by household suffrage—one householder one vote; and (5) that women ratepayers shall have the same right of voting for county as for town councils.

With such a Council in each county, or, in the case of Lancashire and Yorkshire, in each great division of a county, we should have a central local organization, to which highway boards, local boards of health, village school boards, and other small bodies could be affiliated ; and it is not impossible that, as a development of the system, the various bodies controlling the destinies of our lesser towns could be federated to save friction, trouble, and expense ; while, above all, it must be insisted that the representatives of the ratepayers shall have full control over the police.

It is a truism that without good citizens the best of governments must fail ; but our experience of the House of Commons and of the many town councils has shown that the improvement of the machinery and the handing over of control to the great body of the people have brought public-spirited men to the front to do the duties required. As it has been at Westminster and in the towns, so will it be in the counties. England has become greater and freer, our towns have expanded and benefited, owing to the whole of the inhabitants having a direct voice in the rule ; and the counties will correspondingly improve when the same is applied.

# XXII.—HOW IS LOCAL OPTION TO BE EFFECTED?

INTIMATELY connected with the question of county government is that of local option ; and the problem of transferring the licensing power from an irresponsible bench of magistrates to a specially elected body, or to a direct vote of the ratepayers, has ripened towards settlement in a remarkable degree since the day—just twenty years since—when Mr. Gladstone wrote to the United Kingdom Alliance that his disposition was "to let in the principle of local option wherever it is likely to be found satisfactory," and thus used in relation to this question for the first time, as far as is known, a phrase which has become famous.

No leading politician to-day disputes that some form of local option must speedily be provided ; but, as a body, they have been shy of touching a problem that presents a host of difficulties, and the attempt to settle which could not fail to arouse a number of enemies. What those, therefore, who wished for local option have had to do was to show the body of electors that it was reasonable and just, and to trust that their appreciation of these two qualities would lead them to its support.

As to its being reasonable, the very fact that the granting of licences even now is in the hands of the magistrates, and not in those of a Government department, indicates that it is intended that local feeling shall be consulted. This, in fact, was specifically stated in an Act of 1729, which, after reciting that "inconveniences have arisen in consequence of licences being granted to alehouse-keepers by justices living at a distance, and, therefore, not truly informed of the occasion or want of

ale-houses in the neighbourhood, or the character of those who
apply for licences," enacted that "no licences shall in future be
granted but at a general meeting of the magistrates acting in
the division in which the applicant dwells."

Just a hundred years later, Parliament thought fit to withdraw
from the magistrates—who, at the least, knew something of "the
occasion or want of alehouses in the neighbourhood, or the
characters of those who apply for licences"—the power over
applications for beerhouse licences ; and the result showed that
even the most modified form of local option was better than
none. The Act of 1830, "to permit the general sale of beer
and cider by retail in England," provided that "any householder
desirous of selling malt liquor by retail in any house " might
obtain a licence from the Excise without leave from the
magistrates. Within five years another Act had to be passed
demanding better guarantees for the character of those applying
for such licences, the preamble declaring this to be necessary
because "much evil had arisen from the management of
houses " created by the previous statute. Other amending Acts
followed, and in 1882 the magistrates were once more given
complete jurisdiction over beer off-licences, with the result that
in the borough of Over Darwen alone the renewal was at once
refused of 34 out of 72 licences of the kind, a decision which, it
is important to note as bearing upon a point yet to be raised,
was upheld by the Queen's Bench on appeal.

It is not merely a matter of historical interest, but it has very
distinctly to do with the argument in favour of local option, to
show that the magistrates for four centuries have had committed
to them the duty of seeing that the needs of the district were no
more than satisfied. In 1496, a statute directed " against vaca-
bounds and beggers " empowered two justices of the peace " to
rejecte and put awey comen ale-selling in tounes and places
where they shall think convenyent ; " and in 1552 another Act
confirmed this exercise of authority. In 1622, the Privy Council
peremptorily directed the local justices to suppress "unnecessary
alehouses ; " and in 1635 the Lord Keeper, in his charge to the
judges in the Star Chamber previous to their going circuit,
denounced alehouses as " the greatest pests in the kingdom,"

and added this significant hint : " In many places they swarm by default of the justices of the peace, that set up too many ; but if the justices will not obey your charge therein, certify their default and names, and I assure you they shall be discharged. I once did discharge two justices for setting up one alehouse, and shall be glad to do the like again upon the same occasion."

These facts show that the theory upon which our licensing system has grown up is that the wants of a locality shall be strictly borne in mind, and of late years the wishes of a locality have more and more been considered. No one would deny that magistrates as a whole pay greater attention to those wishes to-day than they were accustomed to do even as recently as fifteen years ago ; and when new licences are applied for memorials against their grant, signed by the inhabitants, are allowed to have considerable weight with the bench. But that, after all, is only the result of indirect and irregular pressure. What Local Optionists desire is that the pressure shall be made direct and customary.

The reasonableness of demanding that local wishes shall control the issue of licences is proved by the facts adduced, and the justice is equally capable of being shown. If a locality determines that no fresh licences shall be granted, or that certain old ones shall be taken away, no more injustice will be done than if the magistrates under the present system did the like. No compensation has ever been granted to the holder of a licence the renewal of which a bench has refused ; and although the majority of such refusals has been because of ill-conduct, there have been many cases (and those at Over Darwen were among them) where the magistrates have not renewed because they did not think the house was required. The fact stands that a publican's tenure is in its nature precarious ; he holds his licence from year to year at the pleasure of the magistrates ; he would hold it in the same fashion were Local Option secured. And the fact that the power of refusal to renew a licence would pass from an irresponsible bench to either the whole of the ratepayers or a body specially elected by them for the duty, would not entitle him to demand a compensation then that does not exist for him now.

9

A great difficulty of the problem lies in consideration of the manner in which the popular power shall be exercised. " Local Option " is a somewhat elastic phrase, adopted by many who have never troubled to think what it may involve. Broadly speaking, there are three methods by which it might be carried into effect : (1) By placing the power of licensing in the hands of the Town Councils or the proposed County Councils ; (2) in those of specially-elected licensing boards ; or (3) in those of the ratepayers, who would exercise by ballot a " direct veto."

It is the first plan that finds favour with most of our statesmen. It was prepared to be adopted by the last Liberal Ministry, and is by no means so novel as many suppose. The Municipal Corporations Act of 1835, as originally drawn, contained a clause giving the Town Councils the power of granting alehouse licences, but the proposition was abandoned. The Local Government Bill of Lord Salisbury's Administration has a similar provision, giving the licensing to the County Councils ; but to this has been urged the objection that these bodies will have sufficient business to attend to without having the public-houses placed on their shoulders. When our system of popular education was fixed upon its present basis, it was resolved that the work should be done by specially chosen school boards. Mr. Forster at first proposed that these boards should in the towns be selected by the Municipal Councils ; but it was felt by the House of Commons that so special a function demanded direct election, and direct election was provided, with the best results. And if the licensing power is to be vested in a representative assembly and local option is to be anything but a sham, it must be placed in the hands of those elected by the ratepayers for that special purpose, so that no bye-issues of waterworks, or paving, or the increase of rates shall affect the one distinct question of the public-house.

The extreme temperance section argue that even such Licensing Boards—directly elected by the ratepayers for the specific purpose—would not meet the requirements of the case, and that nothing short of a popular vote can be accepted. But why should the representative system be abolished and a direct vote established in this case, any more than in the equally burning questions settled every day by Parliament, and the lesser but still important matters decided by town councils and school boards ? We in England long ago made up our minds that the most excellent way to get public work done is to choose the best men, give them the requisite authority, and then allow them to do the duty to which they are called. And if we can disestablish a church, revolutionize the land system, or reform our institutions from top to bottom through our representatives, without a direct vote of the people, the question of renewing public-house licences can scarcely demand so exceptional a process as is by some suggested.

My answer, therefore, to the question, " How is Local Option to be worked ? " as well as to the kindred temperance question, " How is Sunday closing to be settled ? " is, " By means of licensing boards, directly elected by the ratepayers." And if this solution be adopted, our licensing system will be placed upon a basis at once more safe and more free from friction or the likelihood of injustice than any other that has been proposed.

# XXIII.—WHY AND HOW ARE WE TAXED?

TAXES are the price we pay for being governed : they defray interest upon money borrowed and wages for protection and service. The fact that they are called by a name which is to many obnoxious, or that they are handed to the State instead of to an individual, ought not to blind us to their real nature --that they are the price of services rendered. The name is nothing. In churches the money we pay is called a pew-rent or an offertory ; in clubs it is a subscription ; to doctors or lawyers a fee ; to tradesmen a price ; to railway companies a fare ; for personal services wages ; for the loan of a house rent ; for life or fire insurance a premium ; and for water a rate. All are in a measure taxes; and if it be answered that the difference is that these payments are voluntary, may not the same be said of much that is called "indirect taxation"?

When the subject is considered, there are three questions which naturally demand reply.

1. Why are we taxed?
2. How are we taxed? and
3. How ought we to be taxed ?

To the first question some answer has already been given. Put in the simplest fashion, the reply would be that it is cheaper to pay taxes and be taken care of than not to pay them and have to take care of ourselves. As members of an organized society, we have to provide for external protection and internal service

for the army and navy as a safeguard against enemies from without, for the officers of the law as a safeguard against depredators within, for the means of government, for education, and for a large number of other matters designed for the security of our persons and property and for the welfare and advancement of the community. We have further to pay the interest upon the National Debt—money borrowed by the State at times of emergency to prosecute such wars as Parliament had sanctioned.

In point of fact, taxes are a substitution for personal service. The State in England once compelled this as a means of raising an army ; and, though this form of personal service was long ago commuted by the payment of a sufficient sum through taxation for the maintenance of a standing force, the State has only waived, not abrogated, the right. Even as lately as the last century people in our country districts had to give six days in the year to the repair of such highways as were under the management of the justices of the peace. In the one case the personal service has been commuted into a tax, in the other into a rate—the difference being that a tax is imperially and a rate locally levied—it being found that forced labour of the kind indicated is more wasteful and less efficacious than hired labour ; and, if any want to know how wasteful and how inefficient, they can find abundant illustrations in the history of the old *régime* in France, or that of the Egyptian fellaheen.

There has been indicated the difference between imperial and local taxation—the one being a tax imposed by the State and the other a rate levied by a local authority. The object in each case is similar ; but, while the cost of the central administration, the army and navy, and the superior courts of justice, with the interest on the National Debt, is paid by taxes, that of lighting, draining, and other purely local matters is defrayed by rates, and that of the police, the poor. the highways, and education comes out of taxes and rates combined.

So much for the *why* of being taxed; let us now consider the *how*. At present the receipts of the State are derived from direct and indirect taxation, together with a form which may be said to come under both these heads. The most familiar mode of direct taxation is the Income Tax ; of indirect, the Customs and Excise; and of that which savours of both, the stamp duties and the profits from the Post Office.

These methods of taxation are, as far as England is concerned, comparatively modern. In the earlier days of settled government in this country, the mode of taxing was different and somewhat fitful, causing much trouble in the collection, and sometimes forming the pretext for revolt. "Aids" to the King were a frequent means of oppression long ago ; and as far back as the time of John they were felt as a grievance, Magna Charta providing that the King should take no aids without the consent of Parliament, except those for knighting the lord's eldest son, for marrying his eldest daughter, and for ransoming the lord from captivity (the lord, it being remembered, holding at that time his land direct from the sovereign). "Benevolences"—a charming name for an unpleasing idea—were also in vogue in the Middle Ages, and, although specifically declared by an Act of Richard III. to be illegal, were levied in a fashion which caused much discontent. "Loans" were another form of raising money which the nation resented, as Charles I. found to his cost ; while a "Poll Tax," as all men know, drove Wat Tyler into rebellion. "Subsidies" and "Tenths" and other taxing devices equally failed in the long run to answer the desired purpose of filling the National Exchequer ; and after the Restoration all such gave place to a system by which the Customs, the Excise, and the Land Tax provided most of the money required.

Gradually the proceeds of the Land Tax dwindled, and direct taxation was almost extinct when, in the throes of the great war with France, which lasted, with slight intervals, for twenty-two years, the younger Pitt revived it in an Income Tax, the form in which it is now mainly known. With the end of the war this ceased, and the proceeds of indirect taxation were again chiefly those upon which the State relied. What the result was, how in every direction trade was hampered and public comfort destroyed, has been summed up for all time in one of Sydney Smith's essays ; and the quotation is worth re-perusal by everybody interested in the subject, and especially by those who to-day are wishing to get rid of the main form of direct taxation we possess—the Income Tax, as revived by Sir Robert Peel.

Uttering, in 1820, a warning to the United States to avoid that spirit which we now call " Jingoism," Sydney Smith wrote —"We can inform Jonathan what are the inevitable consequences of being too fond of glory—TAXES upon every article which enters into the mouth, or covers the back, or is placed under the foot ; taxes upon everything which it is pleasant to see, hear, feel, smell, or taste ; taxes upon warmth, light, and locomotion ; taxes on everything on earth and the waters under the earth—on everything that comes from abroad or is grown at home ; taxes on the raw material ; taxes on every fresh value that is added to it by the industry of man ; taxes on the sauce which pampers man's appetite, and the drug that restores him to health ; on the ermine which decorates the judge, and the rope which hangs the criminal ; on the poor man's salt, and the rich man's spice ; on the brass nails of the coffin, and the ribands of the bride--at bed or board, couchant or levant, we must pay. The schoolboy whips his taxed top ; the beardless youth manages his taxed horse, with a taxed bridle, on a taxed road ; and the dying Englishman, pouring his medicine, which has paid 7 per cent., into a spoon that has paid 15 per cent., flings himself back upon his chintz bed, which has paid 22 per cent., and expires in the arms of an apothecary who has paid a licence of a hundred pounds for the privilege of putting him to death. His whole property is then immediately taxed from 2 to 10 per cent. Besides the probate, large fees are demanded for burying him in the chancel ; his virtues are handed down to posterity on taxed marble ; and he is then gathered to his fathers—to be taxed no more."

Ludicrous as the picture seems, it was correctly painted for the time it depicted ; and it is first to Sir Robert Peel and next to his greatest pupil, Mr. Gladstone, that we owe the change from the harassing indirect taxation of the past to the comparatively innocuous forms of it we have to-day. But it is still from indirect taxation that most of our revenue is derived. The heads of that revenue, as given officially, are—(1) Customs, (2) Excise, (3) Stamps, (4) Land Tax, (5) House Duty, (6) Income Tax, (7) Post Office, (8) Telegraph Service, (9) Crown Lands, (10) Interest on Advances for Local Works and Purchase

Money of Suez Canal shares, and (11) Miscellaneous. Of all
these, Excise stands first by several millions, while Customs are
far ahead of any of the rest, Stamps and Income Tax being
the next best paying sources of revenue.   And, in some form or
other, every one among us—the peer who smokes a cigarette,
the peasant who drinks a pint of beer, and the very pauper who
sends a letter to a friend—has indirectly to contribute his quota
to the Exchequer, while all who earn more than £150 a year
have to pay Income Tax ; and those who inherit property, probate, legacy, or succession duty.

IT being certain that, as long as we are citizens of any sort of State, we shall be called upon to pay for its maintenance, the question "How ought we to be taxed?" is one of considerable moment to all. Grumble we may, but pay we must.

Some think they would solve the problem at a stroke by substituting direct for indirect taxation. They argue that people should know exactly what they are paying for the service of the State; and that direct taxation is not only a more logical but a more economic method of raising the revenue. They show that the consumer of duty-bearing articles pays not only the duty but a percentage upon it as interest to the middleman; and a striking instance of this was afforded in the fact that when, in 1865, Mr. Gladstone, as Chancellor of the Exchequer, took sixpence a pound off the tax on tea, the retail price of that article immediately fell eightpence.

But it may be feared that those who argue in favour of entirely direct taxation make small allowance for the weaknesses of human nature. I may prove to demonstration to the first person I meet that he is paying more than he ought to do because of the working of the indirect system, and that to this wastefulness is added the sin of ignorance as to what he actually does pay; but the chances are ten to one that he will reply that, hating all taxation as the natural man does, he would rather not know to what extent he was being mulcted, and that, if the whole amount were annually and in a lump sum presented to his view, he would never find it in his heart or his pocket to pay it.

To the sternly logical this attitude will appear sad, if not absolutely sinful ; but we have to take man as we find him, and it is of little use attempting to run straight athwart his deepest prepossessions for so small a result as even the substitution of direct for indirect taxation would attain. But there is a further point, which even the political logician must bear in mind, and that is what the practical effect would be of sweeping away all duties of Customs and Excise.

If we could secure a "free breakfast table" by liberating from toll tea, coffee, cocoa, currants, raisins, and other articles of domestic consumption, all would rejoice—though, in the present state of our finances, no Chancellor of the Exchequer is likely to sacrifice the five millions of revenue now raised from those commodities. But the English people will think a good many times before striking tobacco, spirits, and wine off the Customs list, with the more than 13 millions they produce, or spirits and beer off the list of the Excise, with the 13 millions in the one case and the 8½ millions in the other that we now receive from them. Even if any one can imagine for a moment that the 27 millions here involved could be made up by some new direct tax, it does not need an extensive acquaintance with our social history to be aware that the result of removing the duties from the various intoxicants would be widespread national demoralization.

The taxation of the future, therefore, as of the past, will certainly include Customs and Excise. Some items may be struck off both ; that a free breakfast table can be secured should be no dream ; and it may be fairly hoped that the hindrances to trade involved in such licences as those for auctioneers and hawkers—who ought no more to be fined by the Government for practising their employment than butchers, bakers, or other traders—will soon be swept away. But upon beer, wine, spirits, and tobacco—their importation, manufacture, and sale—the tax-gatherer will continue, and rightly continue, to lay his hand.

Similarly, there will be no disposition to abolish the probate, legacy, and succession duties, but every disposition to strengthen them, and especially the last of them. The "Death duties" at present are inequitably levied ; great fortunes do not pay as large a proportion as, relatively to small ones, they ought to do : and landed property is lightly let off compared with other forms.

But it is a comparative few who will be touched even by this much-needed reform ; and taxation, to be fair, must touch all round. The Income Tax, obnoxious as from some aspects all will admit it to be, has almost infinite capacities of being made useful to the State ; and the question which practical statesmen will soon have to consider is the direction in which that usefulness can best be developed.

As at present levied, this tax does not affect those whose incomes are below £150 ; if their incomes are between that sum and £400, the tax is paid upon £120 less than the correct figure ; while if they exceed £400 the full tax is levied.

Now these regulations act unfairly in various directions. In the first place, the tax starts at too high a figure. Until a few years ago it began at an income of £100—a deduction of £80 being allowed—and there is no reason why it should not begin at £50, so that every man earning a pound a week in wages should be made to see as by a barometer how the national expenditure was rising or falling—though it never falls. And, however little he might be called upon to pay, there would be a distinct gain in so many additional capable citizens knowing from experience what an extra penny on the Income Tax means, for they would thereby be taught more closely to watch how the national money is got rid of, and their pockets consequently made the lighter.

In the next place, the regulations now in force make no distinction between a precarious and a settled income, causing the tradesman or professional man, whose revenue dies with him. to pay as heavily as his neighbour who has inherited or acquired property, of which those dependent upon him will not be deprived by his decease. As the point was put in a motion made many years ago in the House of Commons by Mr. Hubbard (now Lord Addington), "the incidence of an Income Tax touching the products of invested property should fall upon net income, and the net amounts of industrial earnings should, previous to assessment, be subject to such an abatement as may equitably adjust the burden thrown upon intelligence and skill as compared with property. Upon this point, it is true, Mr. Gladstone has been antagonistic to the view here held; he opposed this very motion, and years before it was introduced he declared that it was not possible for him to conceive a plan which would secure the desired end. But it is also true that more than thirty years ago, and in his very first Budget speech, he intimated that "the public feeling that relief should be given to intelligence and skill as compared with property ought to be met, and may be met"; and that as plans he could not conceive in 1853 have become realized achievements with him before 1888, this concerning a differentiated Income Tax may yet be added to the number.

The words of Cobden upon the point are as true to-day as when they were uttered. Speaking upon the Budget of 1848, he dwelt upon the inequalities of the Income Tax, which was then still talked of by Chancellors of the Exchequer as a temporary measure. "Make your tax just," he said, "in order that it may be permanent. It is ridiculous to deny the broad distinction that exists between incomes derived from trades and professions, and those drawn from land. Take the case of a tradesman with £10,000 of capital; he gets £500 a year interest, and £500 more for his skill and industry. Is this man's £1000 a year to be mulcted in the same amount with £1000 a year derived from a real property capital of £25,000? So with the cases of professional men, who literally live by the waste of their brains. The plain fair dealing of the country revolts at an equal levy on such different sorts of property. Professional men and men in business put in motion the wheels of the social system. It is their industry and enterprise that mainly give to realized property the value that it bears; to them, therefore, the State first owes sympathy and support."

There is a further injustice under the present system, and that is that, when a man has passed the £400 limit, he has to pay as heavy a percentage upon his income, precarious or permanent, as the wealthiest millionaire among us. The struggling tradesman, the hardly-pressed professional man, every one who depends upon his brains for his living, has to pay as heavily as the Duke of Bedford, the Duke of Westminster, and the Duke of Portland, to whom the brains they possess makes no difference to their income, and whose property has been secured not by efforts of their own, but of others.

Is it any wonder, then, that the demand should be growing for a graduated Income Tax? It is one upon which Mr. Chamberlain has spoken plainly. At Ipswich, in January, 1885, he said— "Is it really certain that the precarious income of a struggling professional man ought to pay in the same proportion as the income of a man who derives it from invested securities? Is it altogether such an unfair thing that we should, as in the United States, tax all incomes according to their amount? . . . Prince Bismarck some time ago proposed to the Reichstag an Income Tax, to be graduated according to the amount of the income, and to vary according to the character of the income. We already have done something in that direction in exempting the very smallest incomes from taxation. But I submit that it is well worthy of careful consideration whether the principle should not be carried a little further." And at Warrington, eight months later, he observed—" I think that taxation ought to involve equality of sacrifice, and I do not see how this result is to be obtained except by some form of graduated taxation— that is, taxation which is proportionate to the superfluities of the taxpayer. When I am told that this is a new-fangled and a revolutionary doctrine, I wonder if my critics have read any elementary book on the subject ; because if they had, they must have seen that a graduated Income Tax is not a novelty in this country. It existed in the Middle Ages, when those who exercised authority and power did so with harshness to their equals, but they knew nevertheless how to show consideration for the necessities of those beneath them."

The first answer to the demand for a graduated Income Tax will, of course, be that it would be " confiscation "—a word by which the rich are ever striving to frighten others from making them pay their proper share to the State ; and one may be content to rest in this matter upon the apparent paradox of Disraeli : " Confiscation is a blunder that destroys public credit; taxation, on the contrary, improves it ; and both come to the same thing." The fact, as has before been stated, is that taxation is the price we pay for protection ; and the more we have to protect, the more we ought to pay.

And, as Mr. Chamberlain observed, this suggestion of a graduated tax is no new-fangled or revolutionary idea : it is one for instances of which it is not even necessary to go back with him to some vague reminiscences of the Middle Ages, for it exists in various degrees at the present time. It is only dwellings of over the annual value of £20 that are liable to inhabited house duty ; houses of less than £30 rateable value have in various districts certain water privileges for nothing which those of greater value have to pay for ; and the difference in the death duties, according to the degree of relationship of the legatee, indicates that the law recognizes the reasonableness of graduating the burden according to the shoulders which have to bear it. And when we come to the Income Tax itself, we find not merely that incomes under £150 are exempt, while those between that sum and £400 are subject to reductions which lessen the percentage of the tax to be paid compared with those above the last given figure, but that no other a Chancellor of the Exchequer than Mr. Gladstone has acknowledged the principle of graduation, and that in the most practical way ; for in his Budget of 1859, when the rate of the tax stood at 5d. and he proposed to add another 4d., he coupled with it the proviso that incomes from £100 to £150 (£100 being the then initial point) should pay only 1½d. extra.

The argument sometimes used that the heavier taxation of large incomes would tend to discourage thrift by putting a penalty upon its results is disposed of by every-day experience. Does a man cease to wish to earn £150 because that sum will make him liable to Income Tax, or £400 because that will bring him fully within its scope ? We know such a man does not exist, and why should the conditions be changed if the graduation went further than at present ?

Here, then, is the claim for a graduated Income Tax, and, after the examples which have been given, it cannot honestly be argued that such a system is either immoral in design or impossible of execution. What is wanted is that the burden of taxation shall be equalized by fixing the greater weight upon the shoulders that ought most to bear it.  No single citizen should be exempt from a share, and by preserving indirect taxation upon luxuries and starting a direct tax at the lowest reasonable point, every one will have to pay something.  But by re-arranging the death duties and graduating the Income Tax we shall secure that those who have most to lose, and, therefore, who demand most from the State, shall pay the State in proportion to their demand.

# XXV.—HOW IS TAXATION TO BE REDUCED?

AT no moment in recent years was it more desirable to urge a demand for retrenchment in the national expenditure, and probably at no moment could such a demand be urged with more chance of good result. For the recent revelations made upon the highest authority as to the wastefulness which characterizes our Government departments have aroused in the public mind not merely indignation at the spendthrifts who rule us but determination to put an end to much of their extravagance.

The only way in which taxation can be reduced is to lessen the need for taxes, and that can be done in no other fashion than by reducing the expenditure. Ministry after Ministry has entered Downing Street with the announced determination to exercise retrenchment, and Ministry after Ministry has left that haven for office-seekers with the expenditure higher than ever. The stock excuse for this state of things is, that as the national needs increase, the national expenditure must increase with them ; but, allowing that this will justify a rise upon certain items, the question which will have to be pressed home to every Minister and would-be Minister, to every member of Parliament and would-be member, is this—" Is the money that is disposed of spent in economical fashion and to the best advantage?" And he will have to be a very thick-skinned specimen of officialdom who will venture to reply " Yes " to the question.

In the estimates for the navy, the army, and the Civil Service, there is abundant room for the pruning knife, while to the principle which underlies the granting of many of the pensions there ought to be applied the axe. Of course, as long as we possess an empire which exceeds any the world has ever seen for the vastness of its extent and its resources, so long must an army and navy be maintained; and even if, by a reverse of fortune, every one of our colonies were cut off from us, an army and navy would still be needed for our own protection. They are as necessary to a nation, situated like our own, as a fire-brigade to a town ; and it would be folly, and worse, to starve them into inefficiency. What money is needed, therefore, to place the defences of the country—whether those defences be men, ships, forts, or coaling stations—in such a state of efficiency as shall avoid the chance of national disaster should war burst upon us, ought to be definitely ascertained and cheerfully granted.

But is the money now voted for the army and navy expended to the best advantage, or is not a large portion of it wasted in useless and ornamental adjuncts? We have not yet reached the point attained by that Mexican force which is traditionally stated to have contained twenty-five thousand officers and twenty thousand men : but the number of superior officers of both services is altogether out of proportion to the size of the force. In order to stimulate what is called the "flow of promotion," officers are placed on the retired list at a ridiculously early age, and the country is deprived of, while having to pay for, the services of those who are in the prime of life, and still capable of doing their full duty, in order that room may be made for their juniors to climb into their places, those juniors themselves being soon supplanted, and the "flow of promotion" going merrily on—at our expense. And the hollowness of the pretension that all this is for the country's good is shown by the fact that, while a determined effort was made by the Horse Guards to compulsorily retire Sir Edward Hamley, the finest tactician England possesses, the Duke of Cambridge is suffered to remain commander-in-chief long after the age at which any other officer would have been shifted. This is only one example of how all rules, salutary and otherwise, are put aside when courtiership demands, for there is a distinct danger, to which the country should be awakened, of our services being royalty-ridden.

Royalty, it is true, has not yet invaded the Civil Service, though the scions of the reigning house are so rapidly increasing in number that the prizes even of this department are likely, at no distant date, to be snatched from the skilled and deserving ; but this particular Government department has plenty to be purged of, notwithstanding. Put in the shortest fashion, the complaint the public have a right to bring against the Civil Service is that it is over-manned and over-paid. A large section of its members—and those located at the various offices in White-hall afford a glaring instance—commence work too late, leave off too early, and even when on their stools have not enough to do. Their number should be lessened, and their hours increased. Ten to four, with an interval for lunch, is a working period so scandalous in its inadequacy that even the Salisbury Ministry has condemned it, and has in some fashion, but at the country's expense, been striving to make it longer. No private business could possibly pay if it adopted such a system ; and what must be done is to treat the Government service upon the same lines as a flourishing private concern. The old notion that a State should provide a maximum of pay for a minimum of work, and that a Government office should be a paradise for the idle and incompetent, must be swept away. It is nothing less than a scandal that taxes should be wrung in an ever-increasing amount from the toilers of the country to pay for work which, under efficient management, could be better done at a less price.

With this question of pay there is linked that of pensions. It is often urged that men join the public service at a less rate of pay than the same abilities could obtain in other walks of business life, not merely because of the security of tenure, but because they know there is a pension to follow the work. This is exceedingly to be doubted ; and although it would be unjust to deprive of pensions those who have entered Government employment under present conditions, the question ought very seriously to be considered whether it would not be wise for the State to pay, as private firms do, for the services actually rendered, and for individual thrift to be allowed to provide for illness or old age. Or, if it be thought desirable to maintain the pension system, the Government servants should be called upon, like the police, to contribute out of their wages to a superannuation fund. The system of pensions, as at present in operation, is indefensible upon sound business principles, and taxpayers have something better to do with their money than continue to spend it for sentimental reasons.

As to hereditary pensions, there is no need to say much. Thanks to Mr. Bradlaugh these are in a fair way to be disposed of ; but it will still need that a keen watch be kept, to prevent the State being further robbed by any fanciful scheme of commutation. It may be taken as settled that no further pensions will be granted for more than one life ; but pensions for a single life, as now arranged, often prove an intolerable burden upon the revenue. A favourite device of the Government offices is to "reorganize" departments, with the result of placing a new set of officials upon the pay sheet and an old set upon the pension list. Many of the latter will be comparatively young men, capable of doing service in other departments ; and, if they are not wanted in one, they ought to work for their pay in another. But that is not the way in which the State does its business. They are pensioned off with such astounding results as was seen in the case of one official, whose place was abolished in 1842, who was pensioned at the rate of nearly £2500 a year, and who lived until 1880 ; or of another, whose office was abolished in 1847, who was pensioned in £3100, and who, up to this date (for he is believed still to be living), has drawn over £120,000 from our pockets without having done a single day's work for the money. And not only is the "reorganization" system a means of lightening the national pocket without good result, but the "ill-health" device has the same effect. Annuitants live long, as all insurance offices will tell you, and it is proved by the fact that there are pensioners still on the list who retired from the Government service between forty and fifty years ago because of "ill-health."

Here, then, are some of the fashions in which the country is defrauded ; they could be multiplied, but the samples should suffice to arouse the attention of all who bewail the continual increase of taxation. The State is evidently regarded by a large section of the population as a huge milch-cow, which shall provide an ever-flowing stream ; and this view will continue to be held as long as our legislators are not forced by the constituencies to give due heed to economy. Nothing practical in that direction can be done until the House of Commons has a thorough control over the national expenditure. At present the control it exercises partakes so largely of the nature of a sham that it is not worth considering ; its scrutiny must become active and persistent, and it should be directed to the pickings secured in high places as well as in low—to the receivers of heavy salaries as well as of light wages. The tendency has too long been to exhibit economy in regard to the small people and to pass over the extravagances which feed the large, and that is a tendency which will have to be stopped.

No one desires to lessen the efficiency of the public service ; but as no one would seriously dream of saying that that quality is at this moment its most distinguishing feature, good rather than harm would be done by the exercise of sound economy. It is only by lopping off the extravagances which have grown up like weeds in our Government departments, and which are now choking much of their power for good, that the taxes can ever be reduced. And so it is the bounden duty of the Liberals to raise their old banner of Retrenchment once again.

# XXVI.—IS FREE TRADE TO BE PERMANENT?

BEFORE leaving the consideration of taxes, the question of Free Trade must be dealt with. A very few years ago it would have been thought as unnecessary to discuss the wisdom of continuing our system of Free Trade as of lengthening the existence of the House of Commons ; but we are to-day threatened with the revival of a Protectionist agitation, and it is necessary to be argumentatively prepared for it.

It is impossible within my limits to say all that can be said in favour of Free Trade or all that ought to be said against Protection ; but it should be the less necessary to do the former, because the proof that it is working evil to the country must rest with those who assert it, and that proof they do not afford.

The main contention of the Protectionists—Fair Traders some of them call themselves, but the old distinctive name is preferable—is that the free importation of corn has ruined agriculture, and of other goods has crippled manufactures. And, having assumed this to be correct, their remedy is to place such a duty upon all imported articles which compete with our own productions as to " protect British industry."

First for the complaint. Is it true that the system of free imports has ruined agriculture and crippled manufactures? There is no doubt that the farming interest has been very seriously hit by a series of inadequate harvests and the growth of foreign competition ; and there is as little doubt that, if such a duty were placed upon imported grain as would make its culture in England profitable under the present conditions, the farmers would thrive, even if the poorer among us starved. No one can deny that, if there is to be Protection at all, the agricultural interest demands it the most, but we will see directly whether such a tariff as would make profitable the growth of wheat is practicable. As to the crippling of manufactures, there is something to be said which is as true as it may be unpalatable. Without denying that the free importation of foreign goods, coupled with the heavy duties levied by other countries upon our exported articles, has seriously diminished the profits of certain of our manufacturers, and has thereby injured the persons by them employed, those who have watched the recent course of British trade are compelled to see that other causes have been at work to account for much of the depression.

Making haste to be rich has had more to do with that depression than the weight of foreign competition. Manufacturers who scamp and merchants who swindle ; folks who endow churches or build chapels to compromise with their conscience for robbing their customers and blasting the honour of the English name—these are the men who deserve to be pilloried when we talk of depression. We *do* want fair trade in the sense of honest trade, for it is the burning desire for gain, the resolve to practise any device that leads to money-making, which is injuring the British manufacturing industry far more than the foreigner. The sick man who disliked a wash was at last, in desperation, recommended by his doctor to try soap ; the manufacturers who size their cottons to the rotting point, and the merchants who have been accustomed to sell German cutlery with a Sheffield label, should be told, when they cry out upon depression, to try honesty. And when they whine, as they sometimes do, that it is the demand for cheap goods that makes such a supply, they must be reminded that the butcher who sells bad meat, or the baker who adulterates his bread, pleads the same excuse, but it does not save either from being branded as a cheat.

There is a further point which will account for the loss of British trade in foreign markets, and that is the lack of adaptability to new circumstances shown by English traders. And this is displayed all round. Our farmers ought to know by this time that they cannot compete by wheat-growing with the United States, Canada, or India ; but they will not comprehend that they can compete with foreign countries in the matter of butter, eggs, cheese, fruit, and poultry. And the consequence is that we are paying many millions yearly to France, Holland, Belgium, and America for articles that our own farmers ought to supply ; and that the largest cheesemongers in London find it cheaper, easier, and quicker to import all their butter from Normandy than to buy a single pound in England. It is the same with our manufacturers. An American firm had a large order to give for cutlery ; they asked terms which the English manufacturer rejected because they were novel ; and a German at once seized the chance, and kept the trade. In New Zealand there was wanted a light spade for agricultural purposes : the English manufacturer would not alter his pattern to suit his customers ; and the whole order went to the United States. In China the people wish for a cotton cloth which will not vanish at the first shower of rain ; Manchester is so accustomed to heavily size its goods that it cannot change ; and the China trade in that commodity is going elsewhere. Before, then, we complain of foreign competition—a complaint which is bitterly heard to-day as against England in France, Germany, Austria, and the United States—let us be certain that we are doing all we honestly can to cope with it.

Some there are who say that they are in favour of Free Trade in the abstract, but that they will not support it as long as it is not accepted by other nations. This is about as sensible as a decision to cheat in business as long as some of our neighbours cheat would be honest, and is exactly on a level with the old death-bed injunction of the miserly parent—"My son, make money—honestly if you can, but make money." And when it is stated, as it sometimes is, that Free Trade was adopted by this country only on the understanding that it would be universally agreed to, it is a sufficient answer that Sir Robert Peel, in introducing his measure for the repeal of the Corn Laws, observed :—" I fairly avow to you that in making this great reduction upon the import of articles, the produce and manufacture of foreign countries, I have no guarantee to give you that other countries will immediately follow our example."

When the Protectionists, call themselves by what name they will and use what arguments they may, ask us to change our present system, we first then deny their assumption that England is going to the dogs, and next we ask what they propose to put in its place. Upon a plan they find it impossible to agree. Some would tax corn lightly, others as heavily as would be required to make its growth certainly profitable to the farmer ; some would fix a duty only upon manufactured articles, others upon everything which is imported that can be raised here ; some would admit goods from our colonies at a lighter rate than from foreign countries, others would put them all on the same level. Out of this chaos of contradictions no definite plan has yet been evolved, and none is likely to be.

The corn question is the first difficulty, and will long remain so. Wheat, in the autumn of 1887, was selling at 28s. a quarter ; on the average it cannot be grown to pay at less than 45s. ; yet it is only a 5s. duty which is being dangled before the farmer. But if he is to lose 12s. a quarter he will be little farther removed from ruin than if he loses 17s. ; he will as much as ever resemble the traditional refreshment contractor who lost a little upon every customer, but thought to make his profit by the number he served ; and the agricultural interest in its wildest dreams cannot imagine that Englishmen are likely to impose a duty raising the price of wheat 60 per cent. A rise of 10 per cent. in the price of bread means a rise of 1 per cent. in the death-rate, and if a duty of 17s. were imposed, that rise would be 6 per cent. What would this mean? That where 100 persons die now, 106 would die then, and the added number would perish from that most awful of all forms of death —death from lack of food. And those extra six would not be drawn from the well-to-do, from the trading classes, or from the ranks of skilled labour, but from those who even now are struggling their hardest for bread, and to whom the rise in price of a loaf from threepence to fourpence three-farthings would mean starvation. For let it never be forgotten that it is upon the poorest that a corn-tax would fall most heavily. The peer

eats no more bread—probably he eats less—than the peasant ;
even when all his family and servants are reckoned, the
quantity of bread consumed is comparatively little more than
in an artisan's household ; but while the peasant and the
artisan would be made to feel with every mouthful that they
were being starved in order that others might thrive, the few
shillings a week that the peer would have to pay would be but
a drop spilt from a full bucket, the loss of which no one could
perceive.

Arising out of the proposal for the re-imposition of a corn-
tax is a consideration which bears upon the idea of levying a
duty upon other imports. India is rapidly becoming more and
more a corn-growing country ; if it were decided to admit its
wheat free, the British farmer would continue handicapped ; if
it were resolved to tax it, India would necessarily retaliate by
protecting its own cotton industries : and what would Lancashire say to that ?

The fact is that, when the proposal to protect industries all
round is considered, the difficulties of securing a feasible plan
are found to be insurmountable. The simplest way, of course,
would be to place a duty upon everything that entered our
ports, and to follow that American tariff which commenced with
a tax upon acorns, and was so jealous of interference with
native industries that it fixed a duty upon skeletons. And if it
be replied that the line should be drawn at manufactured
articles, the question must be asked at once how these are to
be defined. One can understand shoemakers desiring to place a
duty upon foreign-made boots, but they would object to have
the price of leather increased by a tax upon the imports of that
material. The tanner and currier would strongly favour a tax
upon leather, while perfectly willing that hides should be admitted free. But the free importation of hides would affect the
farmer, who would have as much right to protection as either
tanner or bootmaker. And so the price of boots from the
beginning would be raised to everybody, less boots would be
bought, and the whole community, as well as the particular
trades concerned, would suffer. Take the woollen industries
again. Manufacturers might like cloths to be taxed, but would

be willing to see yarns admitted free. Spinners would place a duty upon yarns, but would let wool alone. But the farmer would again step in and demand that the price of his wool should not be lowered by free importation. If Protection is started there is no stopping it ; no line can fairly be drawn between the importation of raw material and manufactured articles ; every trade will want to be taken care of. And we shall be driven back to the time when, in order to protect the farmer, all bodies had to be buried in woollen shrouds ; and, to protect the buckle maker, the use of shoestrings was by law prohibited. More ; we shall be driven back to the period when the artisan and the labourer saw wheaten bread but once a year, when it was barley alone they could afford to eat, and when the rent of the landlord was the one consideration for which Parliament cared, and the welfare of the poor the last thing of which Parliament dreamed.

One can understand why the Protectionist movement should have supporters in high places. There are landlords who are tired of seeing their rents continuously fall, and are as anxious as ever their fathers were to make the community pay the difference between what the land can honestly yield and the return its possessor desires ; and there are manufacturers who are disgusted to find that the days when colossal fortunes could be rapidly made are departing.

It is the duty, therefore, of every Liberal to resist the least approach to a reversal of the present fiscal policy. For it is not a mere question of taxation ; it is not even a question only of money ; it is a question of life and death to the poor. And every man who knows to what a depth of misery Protection brought this country less than fifty years since, and who feels for those who are hardly pressed, will strive to the uttermost against any renewal of the system which, while enriching a few, impoverishes the many, and, to add bitterness to its injustice, involves death by starvation.

# XXVII.—IS FOREIGN LABOUR TO BE EXCLUDED?

ANOTHER of the remedies suggested by political quacks for depression in trade is the revival of the system of "protecting British labour" by preventing the immigration of foreigners—a process which, by the good sense of all Englishmen, has been abolished for centuries.

It is easy, of course, to take what at first sight may seem the "popular" side upon this question. There would be no difficulty in summoning a meeting of English bakers in London, and telling them that they were being ruined because German bakers are overrunning their trade ; or gathering a small army of clerks, and informing them that but for foreign, and particularly German, competition, the native article would have a better chance ; or assembling a serried array of costermongers, and persuading them that, if it were not for Russian, Polish, and German Jews, who swarm the metropolitan thoroughfares with their handcarts, their own barrows would attract more customers. But the whole idea of excluding foreigners because they become competitors is not merely a confession of weakness and incapacity which Englishmen ought never to make, but it is so contrary to the spirit of freedom which has been cherished in this country for ages that no Liberal ought for a moment to give it countenance.

And, to put it on the most sordid ground, where would England and English trade have been had such a principle been acted upon by other countries ? No people in the world has so much benefited by freedom of movement in foreign lands as ourselves. Go where one may, he will find Englishmen to the fore—not only as traders but as workers. What they have done in the colonies and in the United States is patent to all men, but it is not alone in Saxon-speaking lands that they have flourished. If one visits Italy to-day, he will find Englishmen working in the Government dockyards ; when Russia wanted railways it was Brassey and his navvies who made them, and when she needed telegraphs it was English linesmen who stretched the wires ; while in Brazil on every hand English-men are pushing to the front. And there is a lesson to be learned from that passage in the diary of Macaulay, which records how, on a visit to France, he met some English navvies, with the leader of whom he entered into talk : " He told me, to my comfort, that they did very well, being, as he said, sober men ; that the wages were good, and that they were well treated, and had no quarrels with their French fellow-labourers."

China for a long series of ages acted upon the principle of keeping out the foreigner, and upon various pretexts we fought her again and again to secure our own admission. Japan was equally exclusive, and for a longer time ; but even Japan has found out the mistake of trying to live in " a garden walled around." As far back as the date when Magna Charta was signed, the right of foreign merchants to reside and to possess personal effects in England was recognized ; and although the blindness and bigotry of succeeding times banished the Jews in one age and the Flemings in another, we long ago established the right of free entry. It is true that, in the fit of reaction provoked by the French Terror, Alien Acts were passed con-ferring upon the Crown the power of banishing foreigners, but these were superseded half a hundred years ago, and their revival is not to be looked for.

It may be retorted that the United States Congress has taken a different view, for, in addition to various measures adopted in recent years to prevent the immigration of Chinamen, an Act was passed in 1885 " to prohibit the importation and migration of foreigners and aliens, under contract or agreement to perform labour in the United States, its territories, and the district of Columbia." The effect of that measure, coupled with an amending Act adopted two years later, according to English official authority, is "to subject to heavy penalties any person who prepays the transportation, or in any way assists the importation or migration of any alien or foreigner into the said countries under agreement of any kind whatsoever made previously to such importation, to perform there labour or service of any description (with a few exceptions). Masters of vessels knowingly conveying such aliens render themselves liable to fine or imprisonment, and the aliens themselves are not allowed to land, but are returned to the country whence they came."

This law, even if it had not been rendered ridiculous by an attempt to bring ministers of religion within its scope, and even also if it had not proved practically a dead letter, does not, however, go far in the direction of excluding foreign labour. For men of all nations are as free to proceed to the United States to-day as ever they were, the only condition being that they shall not, before landing, have made themselves secure of finding work. If the same law were applied in England, and even if not a single person evaded (as it would be remarkably easy to evade) its provisions, it would not affect one in a hundred of the foreigners who come hither to compete with our own people. Does any one imagine that the German bakers and clerks and costermongers, who are now so much in evidence, have before landing entered into a contract of service?

If they have not, what further measure could be taken? Ought we to pass a law prohibiting every foreigner from landing? Should we add to it the condition that, if he will swear he is a *bonâ fide* traveller, he may be allowed to remain a few weeks under strict surveillance of the police, who will not only watch very carefully that he does no stroke of work while in England, but will see to it that he is promptly expelled when his time is up? Are our customs officers to search incoming ships for aliens as they do for tobacco, and is the penalty for smuggling foreigners to be the same as for smuggling snuff? The project of totally excluding foreign labour would be as impossible of accomplishment as it would be repellent to attempt.

"But," some will answer, "is it right that we should be deluged with foreign paupers, who come upon our rates without paying a penny towards them?" That is quite another matter, and does not affect the question of foreign labour in any but an indirect way. It certainly is not right that we should be burdened by foreign paupers ; and England would be acting in perfect consistence with the principles of liberty and justice if she did as the United States and the Continental countries have done, in prohibiting the landing of paupers, and insisting upon sending them back to the place whence they came. This is a matter of municipal rather than international law ; and a repetition of such a scandal as that of the Greek gipsies, who were excluded from various European ports, and were yet suffered to land here and to become a nuisance and a burden, ought not to be allowed.

What is being argued against is not the enactment of a law to exclude foreign paupers, but of one to exclude foreign workers. But even if the former were to be proposed, it would have to be narrowly watched, lest it should be so drafted as to deprive England by a sidewind of the title of an asylum for the oppressed which she has so long and proudly worn. For it is at the right of asylum that some of the advocates of exclusion wish to strike. In the United States there is being formed a party to strengthen the " Contract to Labour " Law, which avowedly wishes "to stop the import of lawless elements"—an elastic phrase which might cover any body of persons who wished for reform. And in England, Mr. Vincent, the proposer of the Protectionist resolution adopted by the Tory conference at Oxford in 1887, stated that " the indiscriminate asylum afforded here has long been regarded by continental Governments as an outrage on good order and civilization." He may rely upon it, however, that the English love for the right of asylum is not to be destroyed by the wish or the opinion of any despotic Government on earth, and that a right which shook down the strong Administration of Lord Palmerston, when in an evil hour he menaced it at the bidding of Louis Napoleon 30 years since, will withstand the threatenings even of a conclave of chosen Conservatives.

Many things are possible to a Tory Government, and it may be that, in the endeavour to secure some puff of a popular breeze to fill its sails, it will pander to the section which demands the exclusion of foreigners. But how could such a measure be proposed by a Ministry which has among its members the Duke of Portland, whose family name, Bentinck, proclaims his Dutch descent ; Mr. Goschen and Baron Henry de Worms, whose names no less emphatically announce them to have sprung from German Jews ; and Mr. Bartlett, who, though he tells the world by means of reference-books that he was born at Plymouth, forgets to add that this is not the town in England but one in the United States ?

But it is not to be believed that England will in this matter forget her traditions. We, who are descended from Briton and Saxon, from Norman and Dane, have had reason to be proud of our faculty of absorbing all the foreign elements that have reached these shores, and turning them to good account. When our Puritan fathers were hunted down in England, it was in a foreign clime they made their home; when other Englishmen have lacked employment, it is to foreign lands they have gone ; and the hospitality extended to them by the foreigner we have returned. Go into Canterbury Cathedral to-day, and there see the chapel set apart for the French refugees, driven from their country for conscience' sake ; remember how, after the Revocation of the Edict of Nantes, the unhappy Huguenots fled to England to do good service to their adopted country by establishing here the manufacture of silk. Never forget how advantageous it has been for Englishmen to have the whole world open to their endeavours ; and hesitate long before attempting to deny to others that right of free movement in labour which has been and is of such immense advantage to ourselves.

# XXVIII.—HOW SHOULD WE GUIDE OUR FOREIGN POLICY?

BY a natural process of thought, the consideration of the proposed exclusion of foreign labour leads to that of foreign policy generally ; and although the vast questions involved in our external relations are not to be solved in a few lines, an attempt to lay down some general principles upon the matter can hardly be wasted, for of all things connected with public affairs, foreign policy is that of which the average voter knows the least, and for which he pays the most. The yearly twenty-seven millions as interest on the National Debt is a perpetual legacy from the foreign policy of the past ; while an equally turbulent one in the present would increase the already heavy expenditure on the navy and army to an alarming extent. But as all questions covered by the phrase cannot be put in the simple form "Shall we go to war?" there is a necessity for the leading principles which should govern them to be considered.

A good guide to the future is experience of the past, and our English history will have taught us little if it has not shown that many a war has been waged which patience and wisdom might have avoided. And although we have never avowedly gone to war "for an idea," as Louis Napoleon said that France did concerning the expedition in which he stole two Italian provinces, it has been because of the devotion of our statesmen to certain pet theories that much shedding of blood is due.

One of these theories is that some nation or other is "our natural enemy." France for several centuries held that position, and it was as obvious to one generation that the word

"Frenchman" was synonymous with "fiend" as it was for another to link "Spaniard" with "devil" and for a nearer still to consider that the Emperor Nicholas of Russia and "Old Nick" were one and the same. Just now the "natural enemy" idea is happily dormant, if not dead ; but its evil effect upon our foreign policy has been all too plainly marked in many a page of history.

Another theory, and one which has had a more far-reaching extent, is that it is incumbent upon the nations of Europe to maintain "the balance of power." This, again, is a phrase which has lost much of its old force ; but a Continental struggle might cause it to bloom once more with all its baleful effects. Speaking about a quarter of a century ago, Mr. Bright, considering the theory to be "pretty nearly dead and buried," observed of it to his constituents : " You cannot comprehend at a thought what is meant by that balance of power. If the record could be brought before you—but it is not possible to the eye of humanity to scan the scroll upon which are recorded the sufferings which the theory of the balance of power has entailed upon this country. It rises up before me, when I think of it, as a ghastly phantom which during 170 years, whilst it has been worshipped in this country, has loaded the nation with debt and with taxes, has sacrificed the lives of hundreds of thousands of Englishmen, has desolated the homes of millions of families, and has left us, as the great result of the profligate expenditure which it has caused, a doubled peerage at one end of the social scale and far more than a doubled pauperism at the other. I am very glad to be here to-night, amongst other things, to be able to say that we may rejoice that this foul idol—fouler than any heathen tribe ever worshipped—has at last been thrown down, and that there is one superstition less which has its hold upon the minds of English statesmen and of the English people."

The theory which was thus unsparingly denounced held that we, as a nation, have a right to interfere to prevent any other nation from becoming stronger than it now is, lest its increased strength should threaten our interests. Politicians of the old school were accustomed to assure us that, although the name might not have been known to the ancients, the idea was ; and, with that almost superstitious regard which used to be paid to

Greek and Roman precedents, Hume, in one of his "Essays," related that "in all the politics of Greece, the anxiety with regard to the balance of power is apparent, and is expressly pointed out to us even by the ancient historians;" he was of opinion that "whoever will read Demosthenes' oration for the Megalopolitans may see the utmost refinements on this principle that ever entered into the head of a Venetian or English speculatist;" and, having quoted a passage from Polybius, in support of the theory, he observed : "There is the aim of modern politics pointed out in express terms."

But "the aim of modern politics" has been changed within the past century. Since the era which closed with Waterloo in 1815, England, Austria, Russia, France, and Germany have held in turn the dominant power in the councils of Europe, and the balance has been so frequently disturbed that the map-makers have scarcely been able to keep pace with the changes of the frontiers. Look back only thirty years, and see what has occurred. Instead of Italy being "a fortuitous concourse of atoms," or merely "a geographical expression," she is the sixth great Power, the kingdom of Sardinia, the kingdom of the Two Sicilies, the Papal States, the grand duchies of Lucca, Parma, Tuscany, Modena, and the rest, with Venetia (in 1858 an Austrian possession) thrown in, having been combined to form that old dream of Mazzini, Garibaldi, and their fellow-revolutionaries, "United Italy, with Rome for its capital." In the place of a congeries of petty kingdoms and states, always jarring, and with Austria and Prussia ever struggling for the mastery, we see a German Empire, formed by the kingdom of Hanover being swept out of existence, and those of Bavaria, Saxony, and Wurtemburg, with various grand duchies, placed under the domination of Prussia. In the same period Russia has gained and France has lost territory ; the Ottoman Empire has been "consolidated" into feebleness ; and the kingdoms of Roumania and Servia, with the principality of Bulgaria, have been called in their present shape into being. All this has seriously disturbed the "balance of power ;" but what could England have done to hinder the process if she had wished, and what right would she have had to attempt it if she had dared ?

And in addition to the disturbance of the " balance of power " by process of war and revolution, there is that which comes from physical, educational, industrial, and moral causes. Some nations have a greater faculty than others of securing success in the markets of the world, and these develop their natural resources in such fashion as to outstrip their neighbours. If we ought to be continually fighting to prevent other countries from aggrandizing themselves in point of territory, we ought equally to do so to hinder them from becoming disproportionately powerful in point of wealth. But as there is no man among us so insane as to suggest the latter, so, it may be hoped, will there soon be none to instigate the former. It is now over twenty years since even a Tory Administration felt constrained to omit from the preamble of the Mutiny Bill some words relating to the preservation of the " balance of power " ; and if anything had been needed to cast undying ridicule upon the theory it was the plea of King Milan that he went to war with Prince Alexander in 1885, because the union of Bulgaria with Eastern Roumelia had disturbed the " balance of power " in the Balkan States.

Another idea upon which it is often sought to provoke war is " regard for the sanctity of treaties." There is an honest sound about this which has caused it to deceive many worthy folk, but who in his heart believes that there is any " sanctity " about treaties ? Nations, as a fact, abide by treaties just as long as it suits their purpose, and not a day longer. Take the Treaty of Vienna, which after 1815 was to settle the affairs of Europe for ever. The disruption of Belgium from Holland was the first great blow at its provisions, and one after another of these subsequently became a dead letter. The Treaty of Paris, concluded after the Crimean War, Russia deliberately set aside in a most important part as soon as she conveniently could. The Treaty of Frankfort, between Germany and France, will last only as long as the French do not feel themselves equal to the task of wresting back Alsace-Lorraine. And the Treaty of Berlin, the latest great European compact of all, entered into after the Russo-Turkish War, has already been violated in various directions, and is daily threatened with being violated in more. A treaty, in fact, is not like an agreement between equal parties, in which one gives something to the other for value received ; it is customarily a bargain hardly driven by a conqueror as regards the conquered, and one from which the latter intends to free himself as soon as he has the chance. And so, whenever any one talks about the "sanctity of treaties," let us first see what the treaties are, and under what circumstances they were obtained. It will then be sufficient time to consider the amount of reverence which is their due.

But there is a further theory upon which war is made, and that is the most sordid of all, for, discarding all notions of honour and glory, it simply avers that we ought to physically fight for commercial advancement. A recent writer who seeks to tell us all about " Our Colonies and India ; how we got them, and why we keep them," devotes his first chapter to attempting to prove that nothing but desire for gain actuated our forefathers in every one of their great wars, or, to use his own illustration, " we were afraid that our estate was going to be broken up ; we had a large family ; and we spent money and borrowed money to keep the property together, and to extend it. From our point of view, as a nation, we have to set one side of our account against the other and see whether our transaction paid. It is," he adds, "very often said that England has very little to show for her National Debt. Nothing to show for the National Debt ! It is the price we pay for the largest Colonial Empire the world has ever seen." This is probably the most naked exposition of the worst side of the saying that " Trade follows the flag " which has in late years been published ; but that the idea which underlies it still actuates a certain school of statesmen is shown by the fact that Lord Randolph Churchill justified the expedition to Upper Burmah—as long, tedious, and destructive a business as it was promised to be short, easy, and dangerless—on the ground that the new territory would "pay."

Now here are certain principles which have guided the foreign policy of the past, and which stand as beacons to warn us against dangers in the future. That we shall escape war for all time to come is not to be hoped for, but, by considering the crimes and blunders and bloodshed which have flowed from previous methods, something may be done to avoid it.

# XXIX.—IS A PEACE POLICY PRAC-
# TICABLE?

THE question whether a settled adherence to the principles of non-intervention is compatible at once with our interests and our honour is one upon which much of the future of England may depend. The answer is not to be found in sneers at a " peace-at-any-price policy," which has never been adopted by any section of our countrymen, or in panegyrics upon the virtues evolved by war, made by men who sit comfortably in their arm-chairs while they hound others on to bloodshed. It is a question which of necessity can only be answered in certain cases as the circumstances arise, but there is nothing either cowardly or dishonourable in considering the general principles involved in a reply.

Looking at the world as it stands, it seems almost beyond hope that war will ever cease. It is true that we have got rid of blood-letting in surgery and that we have got rid of blood-letting in society, and it may, therefore, seem to some that there is a chance of getting rid of blood-letting between States. A century since, the doctor's lancet and the duellist's pistol were rivals in slaughter, and all but fanatics thought their abolition impossible. What will be said of war in the time to come?

Whatever may be said of it then, we know what can be said of it now. It is a grievous curse to the nations engaged, and a calamitous hindrance to civilization. It is a barbarous and illogical method of settling international disputes, which decides only that one side is the stronger, and never shows which side is the right. · The cynical saying that God is on the side of the big battalions is true at bottom. We laugh to-day at the old custom of " Trial by battle," recognizing that the innocent combatant was often the weaker or less skilful, and that the guilty consequently triumphed. But " Trial by battle," as between nations, is equally absurd, if any one imagines that it shows which is the righteous. Who would contend that France was in the right when Napoleon Bonaparte, in his early career, by his superior skill in tactics, swept the nations of Europe before him at Arcola and Marengo, Austerlitz and Jena, and that he was in the wrong when, in the waning of his powers, he was irretrievably ruined at Waterloo? That Denmark was in the wrong because the combined forces of Austria and Prussia crushed her in the struggle over Schleswig-Holstein, and that Prussia was in the right when, after she and her neighbour had quarrelled like a couple of thieves over their booty, she placed the needle-gun against the muzzle-loader and overwhelmed Austria? The spirit which impels each combatant to call upon the Almighty as of right for assistance, and which leads the victor to sing a *Te Deum* at the struggle's close, is a blasphemous one, which should not blind us to the criminality of most wars. To hurl thousands of men into conflict in order to extend trade or acquire territory is an iniquity, disguise it by what phrases we will. In private life the man who steals is called a thief, the man who kills is called a murderer ; why in public life should the nation which steals, and which kills in order to steal, be differently treated ? If there be retributive justice beyond the grave, Frederick the Great and Napoleon Bonaparte, who in cold blood and for selfish motives sacrificed tens of thousands of lives, will stand at the murderers' bar side by side with those lesser criminals who have gone to the gallows for a single slaughter.

Let us look at war, therefore, as it is—a direful necessity, even when justified by self-preservation, a flagrant crime when entered upon for the extension of territory or trade. It is easy to raise the cry of patriotism whenever a war is undertaken, but the patriotism that pays others to fight is a cheap article which deserves no praise. As for the bloodthirsty bray

of the music halls, which even English statesmen have not
disdained to stimulate in favour of their policy, it is abhorrent
to cleanly-minded men ; the ethics of the taproom and the
patriotism of the pewter-pot are not to their taste ; and when
it is seen that the most sanguinary writers and the most blatant
talkers are the last to put their own bodies in peril, it cannot
but be concluded that their theory is that patriotism is a virtue
to be preached by themselves and practised by their neighbours.

But though a reckless or merely aggressive war is not only
the greatest of human ills but the gravest of national crimes,
an armed struggle is in certain instances a necessity. Self-
preservation is the first law of nature ; and as no man would
condemn another for slaying, if no milder measure would do,
one who attempted to kill him, and the law would regard such
a course as justifiable homicide, so a nation is right to fight
against invasion, and would deserve to be extinguished or
enslaved if it did not. "Defence, not defiance," the motto of
our volunteers, should be the motto of our statesmen ; and
then, if an enemy attacked us, we should be able to give a good
account of ourselves.

In order to act up to this motto, we must dabble as little as
possible with affairs that do not directly concern us. We should
cease to think that we are the arbiters of the world's quarrels—
we have enough to do to look after our colonies and ourselves
—and we should withdraw from such entangling engagements
as we have, and enter upon no fresh ones. When, for instance,
we are urged to formally join the Triple Alliance, we must ask
why we should bind ourselves to fight France and Russia
because Germany would like to pay off old scores, Austria
wishes to get to Salonica, and Italy is eager to assert her position as the latest-created "Great Power." As it is, a Continental struggle, such as is bound to come in the near future,
may sufficiently involve us. No one seems quite to know
whether we are or are not bound by treaty to defend the
territorial independence of Belgium ; but as it is through "the
cockpit of Europe" that Germany may next attempt to assail
France, or France try to reach Germany, the question is a

very important one. Would it not be better to settle that before we proceed to bind ourselves with the chains of an alliance which could do us little good, but might easily effect considerable harm ?

Non-intervention has again and again been proved to be an honourable and beneficent policy. There has been scarcely a great war within the last thirty years in which we have not been urged by some section in this country to interfere. The Franco-Austrian conflict in 1859, the civil war in America, the Austro-Prussian attack upon Denmark, the Franco-German war, and the Russo-Turkish struggle—in every one of these we were urged to interfere on behalf of our interests or our honour,  · or both. In none did we do so, and who to-day will argue that abstention was wrong ? There are some politicians who appear wishful to see England's finger in every international pie, and the same old arguments, the same vehement appeals, are used whenever there is a struggle abroad. And when the next occurs, and these weather-beaten arguments and appeals are again brought to the fore, let those who may be swayed by them turn to the files of the newspapers which instigated intervention in all of the cases named ; and let them reflect that non-intervention proved the best course in every one, and that what did so well before is most likely to do well again.

But, even if we sedulously pursue this policy, there are occasions when differences arise with other States, and the question is how these can be composed. In the large majority of cases the remedy will be found in arbitration. Here, again, we shall be confronted with assertions about honour and patriotism, which experience has proved to be worthless. Two striking instances have been afforded of the value of international arbitration. The greater is that which solved the difficulty between ourselves and the United States concerning the Alabama claims. Here was a matter in which England was distinctly in the wrong, and, as long as the sore remained open, so long was there danger of war ensuing between the two great English-speaking nations of the earth. When Mr. Gladstone's first Government resolved to submit it to arbitration, no language was too vehement for some of our Tories to apply to the process. It was dishonourable, unpatriotic, and pusillanimous; but Mr. Gladstone persevered, and with what result? The dispute was settled, the sore was healed; and is there a solitary man among us who will contend that the better plan would have been to send into their graves thousands of unoffending men, and to perpetuate, perhaps for generations, a quarrel which has been so happily decided as now to have almost faded out of mind? The other instance is afforded by the resolve, in the spring of 1885, to refer the dispute with Russia concerning the Penjdeh conflict to arbitration. There were threatenings of slaughter on every hand, for weeks there appeared a danger of our being launched into war for a strip of Afghan territory, worthless alike to Russians, Afghans, and ourselves, and upon a conflict of testimony as to the original aggression, which even yet has not been composed. The agreement to submit the matter to the King of Denmark, though his arbitrament ultimately was dispensed with, gave a breathing time to Russia and England both; and who now would argue that we ought to have gone to war because of Penjdeh?

Therefore, if we adhere to a policy of non-intervention in disputes that do not directly concern us, and of arbitration in those in which we become involved, we shall be following a course which the immediate past has proved to be not only peaceful but honourable and agreeable to our interests. "The greatest of British interests is peace," once observed the present Lord Derby; and the truth of the saying is unimpeachable. And when we are told that, strive as we will, war sometimes must come, one is reminded of the saying of a far greater statesman than Lord Derby, and one upon whose patriotism none has been able to cast a slur. It was Canning who, when told that a war in certain circumstances was bound to come sooner or later, replied, "Then let it be later."

If, however, we wish England to pursue a peaceful policy, we must teach the people to believe that it is as honourable as it is practicable, and as truly patriotic as both. It is a mistake to think that the masses will oppose war merely because of the suffering and loss it entails; there are considerations beyond these which the artisan feels as keenly as the aristocrat, the peasant as the peer. The sentiment which resents, even to blood-shedding, an insult to the national flag, may be often to be deprecated but never to be despised ; for when the people shall care nothing for the country's honour, the days of independent national existence will be drawing to a close. And, therefore, when it is argued that a peace policy is practicable, it is held to be so only because it is honourable, patriotic, and just.

# XXX.—HOW SHOULD WE DEAL WITH THE COLONIES?

THE foreign relations of England are necessarily complicated by her colonial concerns ; and these deserve the most careful consideration, because at any moment they may arouse the hottest political dispute of the day. In considering the colonies we have to ask three questions : (1) How and why did we get them ; (2) How and why do we keep them ; and (3) Ought we to force them to stay ?

At the history of the why and how we acquired our colonies, it is impossible here to do more than glance. By settlement as in the case of Australasia, by conquest as in that of Canada, and by treaty cession as in that of the Cape, have been obtained within the past three centuries practically all that we have. The wish for expansion has continually made itself felt, and the frequent result of war as well as of peaceful discovery has been to gratify it. And the consequence of both conquest and discovery has been the acquisition of a colonial empire vaster in extent and resources than the world has ever seen.

Having got our colonies, there are various reasons for retaining them. The imperial spirit, which is elated by expansion and would be deeply wounded by contraction, has been a prominent factor in causing England to take a leading position in the world's affairs ; and it is one which none interested in her prosperity will despise. Even if there were no material reasons for keeping our colonies, this sentiment would cause many Englishmen, and probably the majority, to regard with the deepest distrust any movement having a tendency to separate the colonies from the mother country.

But there are material reasons for binding the colonies to us which none will ignore. They form not only an outlet for our surplus labour and enterprise, but give us markets of high importance to our trade. Emigrants who go to Canada or Australia not merely remain attached by obvious considerations to the English connection, but continue to be our customers in a very much larger degree than if they went to the United States or any other foreign country. Those who study the statistics of our export trade will recognize that if we lost the custom of our colonies—and this we should be likely to do if we lost the colonies themselves—the consequences to our commerce would be very serious.

Thus there are reasons of the highest sentiment, as well as of commercial expediency, for retaining the possessions the hard fighting and determined enterprise of many generations of Englishmen have acquired; but the question which is needed to be answered in much more fulness than either of the others is that which may affect the politics of the near future : Ought we, if any of our self-governing colonies desire to secede, to force them to stay ?

A distinct différence has been made in the form of this question between the self-governing colonies and the dependencies —a distinction arising from the very nature of things. There is a chasm between the consideration of letting Australia or letting India go, which is too wide to be bridged. Australia consists of various colonies, peopled by Englishmen or the descendants of Englishmen, who have the fullest means of constitutionally expressing their desires. India has a vast concourse of deeply-divided peoples, who have no bond of union, whether of race, religion, or common descent, and who are in no sense self-governed. In the argument about to be set forward, therefore, it is to be understood that only the colonies, and not the dependencies, are in consideration.

Broadly speaking, it may be submitted with regard to our self-governing colonies that we are bound in honour to keep them as long as they will stay, and in conscience not to detain them when they are able and willing to go. Having acquired them, and given the most practical guarantees to protect them, we ought to hold to our implied bargain at any cost, and to defend them with as much energy as our native soil. But, just as a parent's duty to a child is to do everything to protect and assist him in his period of growth, so is it equally his duty, when the training-time has been accomplished, to set no hindrance in the path of his acquiring an independent position. And the relation of parent to child has a true likeness to that of England to her self-governing colonies.

If it be asked whether this question of what should be done in case of a proposed separation ought to be raised at the present moment, the reply is that events are forcing the matter forward, and that it is well to consider in a time of comparative quiet a problem which may convulse the nation from end to end if urged upon us in a storm.

For rumblings of the storm have already been heard from the three great self-governing portions of our colonial empire. Sir Henry Parkes, the Premier of New South Wales, in an article published no long time since, and in the very act of proposing a scheme by which he imagined the mother country and the colonies might be knit more closely together, uttered a warning that separation might within the next generation be pushed to the front, for "there are persons in Australia, and in most of the Australian Legislatures, who avowedly or tacitly favour the idea." And he added : "In regard to the large mass of the English people in Australia, there can be no doubt of their genuine loyalty to the present State, and their affectionate admiration for the present illustrious occupant of the throne. But this loyalty is nourished at a great distance, and by tens of thousands, daily increasing, who have never known any land but the one dear land where they dwell. It is the growth of a semi-tropical soil, alike tender and luxuriant, and a slight thing may bruise, even snap asunder, its young tendrils."

When we turn from Australia to Canada, the same warning is in the air. In the autumn of 1887, the remarks of Mr. Chamberlain at Belfast, repudiating the principle of commercial union between Canada and the United States, evoked strong protests from some leading newspapers in the Dominion against the idea of England interfering if such a union were agreed upon. The Toronto *Mail* put the matter in a nutshell when it observed—" Let there be no misunderstanding on this point. Canadians have not ceased to love and venerate England, but have simply reached that stage of development when their choice of what is best for themselves, be it what it may, must prevail over all other considerations." Should it be said that this is only an utterance of our old friend "the irresponsible journalist," it may be added that the practice of Canadian statesmen appears to be in accordance with the principles of Canadian writers. This was certainly the opinion of our own *Standard*, which, in an article in 1887 upon the increases in the Canadian tariff directed against imported iron and steel, wrote—" The obvious truth of the matter is that Canada has given no thought to our interests at all, but only to her own. . . . Of course these Canadians are a most 'loyal' people for all that, and if they can get us to lend them our money they will flatter us and heap sweet-sounding phrases upon us, till the most voracious appetite for such is cloyed to sickness. It is only when we expect them to pay us our money back, or at least to put up no barriers against our trade with them, that we find out how hollow these phrases are. No federation of the empire can take place under any guise while its leading colonies, which love us so exceedingly, strive their utmost to injure our trade. . . . Why should we waste a drop of our blood or spend a shilling of our means to shelter countries whose selfishness is so great that they never give a thought to any interest of ours? That is the question the Protectionist colonies are forcing Englishmen to ask themselves, and it is as well that it should be bluntly put to them now."

Cape Colony is as ready as Australia or Canada to resent the least interference from the mother country. Sir Gordon Sprigg, its Premier, referring at a public meeting late in 1887 to a Bill which the Imperial Ministry had been asked to disallow, observed that, if it should be disallowed, it was not a question of this particular Bill, but whether the colony was to have a free government, or whether necessary legislation in South Africa was to be checked by irresponsible persons at home, and they were to go back to the old Constitution, and be governed by a people six thousand miles away, knowing little of the requirements of the inhabitants of the Cape.

Therefore, we have to face a growing opinion among the self-governing colonies that they will allow England no controlling voice in their internal affairs ; and the question will present itself to many Englishmen whether it is right that we should be saddled with the responsibility of defending colonies which resent any interference, and use their tariffs to lessen our trade. As long as they require help we are bound in honour to give it ; but when they demand, as at some time they will demand, separation, the conviction they are now impressing upon us that they can do without England, will materially strengthen the desire to say to them, " Go in peace."

Even if such a consideration did not exist, one might hope that England would never repeat the enterprise once attempted against what are now the United States, and try to crush a growing nation of our own children when wishing to take its own place in the economy of the world. Some will answer that all danger of such a contingency would be avoided by the adoption of a sound plan of imperial federation ; but where is that sound plan to be looked for ? Even the most ardent advocates of the principle do not venture upon a plan. They are content to talk of sympathy rather than develop a system ; but sympathy does not go far when practical considerations are concerned. It may be argued that sympathy went a long way when a detachment from New South Wales assisted our military operations in the Soudan ; but the experiment was a dangerous one which ought not to be often repeated. Franklin in his autobiography tells us that it was the defeat of Braddock's force which first taught the American colonists that it was possible to hope for independence ; and the lesson needs remembering.

What those who advocate imperial federation have to prove is that it is practicable to persuade each portion of this vast empire to pay and to fight for every other portion. As long as England does both the paying and the fighting, things may go smoothly. But if England went to war with France over the New Hebrides, in order to protect the interests of Australia, what would Newfoundland say on being asked to share the

bill? Similarly, if England engaged France over the bait question, so as to preserve the fishing trade of Newfoundland, how
would Australia like to be taxed for the fray? And if we fought
the United States on the fisheries dispute in order to please
Canada, does any one imagine that Australia or Cape Colony
would agree to additional imposts for the lessening of our
National Debt? It is when considerations like these are discussed that imperial federation appears a pleasing dream rather
than a probable reality.

And, therefore, when we discuss our future dealings with the
colonies, we ought to know how far we intend to go. As long
as they remain with us, we ought to do our utmost to preserve
the most friendly relations ; but, having given them self-government, we ought to impress upon them the necessity for self-
preservation. And if, when they can not only rule but protect
themselves, they should ask to be freed from even the nominal
allegiance to the English Crown which is all they now give, they
should be suffered to go, in the hope and belief that they would
prosper.

# XXXI.—SHOULD THE STATE SOLVE SOCIAL PROBLEMS?

THOUGH we have been discussing at this length our foreign and colonial relations, we must never forget that there is a "condition of England question" which claims the closest attention. The politics of the future will be largely coloured by considerations arising from our social developments ; and it is important to decide whether the State ought to attempt to solve social problems, and how far it ought to interfere in the relations between man and man.

There is just now so much talk about Socialism that it is desirable to examine the principles which underlie State-interference with private affairs. Those who like to divide men into strictly defined parties are accustomed to describe their fellows as Socialists and Individualists ; and, although there is no Socialist who would prevent all liberty of personal action, and no Individualist who would protest against every form of State-interference, the distinction is fair enough if it be understood that the Socialist believes that the State should do as much as possible, and the Individualist that it should do as little as possible, for those who dwell within its limits.

The view of the former is concisely stated in the programme of the Social Democratic Federation, in which are urged the immediate compulsory construction of healthy artisans' and agricultural labourers' dwellings, free compulsory education for all classes, with at least one wholesome meal a day in each school, an eight hours' working day, cumulative taxation upon all incomes above a fixed minimum, State appropriation of

12

railways with or without compensation, the establishment o national banks absorbing all others, rapid extinction of the National Debt, nationalization of the land, and organization of agricultural and industrial armies under State control on co-operative principles. These are merely claimed to be palliative measures, which should be followed by others more drastic ; but they suffice to show the present-day Socialistic idea.

Against this extreme Socialist view must be set the extreme Individualist, which has been expressed by Mr. Spencer, who says—"There is reason to believe that the ultimate political condition must be one in which personal freedom is the greatest possible, and governmental power the least possible ; that, namely, in which the freedom of each has no limit but the like freedom of all ; while the sole governmental duty is the main-tenance of this limit." And the main idea of this statement had been anticipated in the remark, a couple of thousand years ago, by one of the greatest of Greek philosophers—"The truth is that the State in which the rulers are most reluctant to govern is the best and most quietly governed, and the State in which they are most willing is the worst."

The real question, of course, is not between any such extreme views, for Mr. Spencer would not deny that the State sometimes must interfere, and Mr. George would be the last to plead against the use of all individual effort. But though the limits of State-interference are what we have to determine, it is neces-sary first to consider whether the State should interfere at all.

An obvious answer is that the State interferes already in many a social problem, and that no one seriously proposes to do away with that interference. But even those who would thus reply may not be aware of the extent to which the State makes its influence felt in social affairs. The administration of justice and the protection of the commonwealth are necessarily, in all civilized communities, the affair of the State. But beyond these limits, the ruling authority, whether exercised through imperial or local officials, wanders at many a point.

The Poor-law is a striking instance of this fact, for it is a piece of legislation the Socialistic tendency of which none can gainsay, the State practically asserting that no one need starve, and providing food and shelter, under certain conditions, for all who are unable, or even unwilling, to work. The system of national education is another instance of Socialistic legislation; it makes me pay towards the education of my neighbour's child, not for any immediate benefit to myself, but for my ultimate benefit as a citizen of an improved State. And the ruling authority goes further even than compelling me to feed the poor and educate the young, for it interferes, presumably for my good, with my liberty in many a detail.

From birth to death the State, even under present conditions, steps in at point after point to direct one's path. Within forty days of being born I am compelled by the State to be registered; within three months I am equally constrained to be vaccinated; from five years old to thirteen, with certain limitations, I have to be sent to school; and, should my parents be so sensible as to apprentice me to a trade, a fee has to be paid to the State for the indentures. When I marry it is at a State-licensed institution; when I die it is by a State-appointed officer that my decease is certified. And in the interval, the State prevents me from obtaining intoxicating liquor except from certain individuals and within specified hours; it compels me, if I am a house-owner, to effect my sanitary arrangements in a given way; and if I am a house-holder, to keep my pavement free from snow. From the highest details to the lowest, then, the State even now interferes; whether I fail to have my child vaccinated or my chimney swept, it steps in; and those who argue that Individualism is a theory so true that State-interference should be abolished, have a number of fruits of that State-interference to get rid of before they can claim the victory.

But probably even those who imagine that they are extreme Individualists would not wish to remove from the Statute Book such specimens of State-interference as are now upon it. If they did, the clearance would indeed be great. For imagine what the effect would be if, in addition to the other measures indicated, we got rid of all the enactments affecting labour, and again allowed the employment of climbing boys as chimney-sweeps, of women and small children in mines, of men and women in white-lead works without precaution of any kind, of sailors in the merchant service without the protection of lime-juice against scurvy and of survey against sinking ; picture what the population of our manufacturing districts would by this time have become without the protection afforded by the Factory Acts ; remember what an improvement has been made in the way of guarding dangerous machinery, owing to the penalties inflicted upon careless owners by the Employers' Liability Act ; and then answer whether State-interference is necessarily a bad thing.

Within the limits which experience has shown to be desirable, it is a good thing ; and it is no answer to this assumption that it has sometimes failed to secure the object aimed at. As long as nothing in this world is perfect, we cannot expect the action of the State to be ; the only test in every case is an average test. If such State-interference as we see has on the whole done well, the balance must be struck in its favour ; and in human affairs a favourable balance is all we have a right to anticipate.

The Individualistic ideal may be a good one, but it is the Individualistic real we have to examine. And what would become of the poor, the weak, and the helpless if the State stood aside from all interference with the affairs of men ? That the rich and the powerful would grind them to powder in their struggles for more riches and greater power. The days of universal brotherhood have never existed—and, what is more, never will exist—and that State which protects the weak against the strong and the poor against the rich is the best worth striving for.

An ideal condition of society would be that in which every able-bodied person would have to work for a living with body, brains, or both ; but birth and bullion play so large a part under present circumstances that, while we may sigh for the ideal, we must recognize the real. And this applies to all thinkers on our social affairs—to the extreme Socialist as to the extreme Individualist. The mystery of life cannot be solved by logic, and the pain, the poverty, and the crime which that mystery involves dissipated by law.

It must constantly also be borne in mind that mankind is not governed by material considerations alone, but is largely swayed by sentiment ; and any system which ignores this and treats men simply as calculating machines is bound to fail. Thus it is that, while men accept the latest doctrines of social science, they do not act upon them. They sympathize with Mr. Spencer's account of an ideal State in which the governmental power is the least possible, but they pay the education rate, support compulsory vaccination, and express not the slightest wish to see public-houses open all night. It is in this as in other theoretical affairs—our minds agree, but our hearts arbitrate. A parent may accept most thoroughly the doctrine of the survival of the fittest, but he will strive his utmost to preserve life to a crippled or lunatic child. And a trader may indicate assent when he hears that the employed ought to be paid only the amount which would secure similar services in the labour market ; but, if he is even commonly honest in his dealings with his fellows, he will not discharge an old servant because he can obtain another for something less.

But no sooner do some men secure a fact than it begets a theory, and truth thus becomes the father of many lies. It is well enough that every one should strive to be independent of external help, but it is not within the bounds of the possible that every one can be perfectly so ; and that being the case, the State, as the protector of all, is bound to interfere. What has to be decided is the limit of such interference ; and although upon that point no precise line can be drawn, for as conditions vary so must the limit change, discussion may serve to show that all the truth lies in neither of the contending theories, but in a judicious use of both.

# XXXII.—HOW FAR SHOULD THE STATE INTERFERE?

To precisely limit the interference of the State in private affairs has been urged to be impossible, for the boundaries of such interference are ever changing, and will continue ever to change as the circumstances vary. In some respects the State has more to say about our domestic concerns, in others less, than it formerly had ; but there never was a time when it left us altogether alone, and there is never likely to be.

When people groan about "grandmotherly government," and talk hazily of "good old times" when such was unknown, they speak with little knowledge of the social history of England. They forget that there was a day when under penalty men had to put out their fires at a given hour ; that later they were directed to dress in a fashion presumed to be becoming to their several ranks ; that at one period they had to profess Catholicism under fear of the fagot, and at another Protestantism under penalty of the rope ; that in later days they had to go to church to escape being fined, and even until this century had to take the Sacrament in order to qualify for office ; that in other times they were allowed to bury their dead only in certain clothing ; that a section of them had to give six days in the year to the repair of the highways ; and that in divers further ways their individual liberty was fettered in a fashion which would not now be tolerated for a day.

The State, in fact, has always claimed to be all-powerful, and has never assigned set limits to its demands. It has asserted, and still asserts, rights over that which is intangible, which it has not created, and which in its origin is superhuman. If a man has used a stream for his own purposes for a given period, the State secures him a right of use, protecting him from interference in or providing him compensation for that which neither he nor the State made or purchased. If another has a window which is threatened with being darkened by a newer building adjacent, the State steps in to assure him of the retention of his "ancient light." And when people have for a series of years walked without hindrance across land belonging to others, the State gives to the commonalty a right of way, which, however seemingly intangible, often seriously deteriorates the value of the property over which it is exercised.

In the gravest concerns of man as well as in those which merely affect his comfort or his purse, the State intervenes. It used to assert by means of the press-gang its right to seize men for service in war ; and it could at this day order a conscription which would compel all in the prime of life to pass under the military yoke. It can and does direct property to be seized for public purposes, upon compensation paid, from an unwilling owner ; and it can and does take out of our pockets a proportion of our income, which proportion it has the power to largely increase, in order to pay its way.

That which does all these things is for convenience called "the State," but in present circumstances it is really ourselves. The nation is simply the aggregate of the citizens who compose it, and each one of us—especially each possessor of a vote—is a distinct portion of the State. The misfortune which attends upon the frequent use of the word is that many persons seem to think that there is some mystic power called "the State" or "the Government," which can dispense favours, spend money, and do great things—all from within itself. But neither State nor Government has any money save that which we give it, and no power except that which is accorded by the constituencies. And, therefore, when people cry out for "the State" to do this or "the Government" to do that, they should remember that *they* are portions of the force they beseech, and that if what is to be done costs money they will have to pay their share ; and this much it is highly useful to recollect when appeals are more and more being made to the State for help.

Let us start, therefore, with the conviction that the State, which is simply ourselves and others like us, has no power beyond what the people give it, and no money but what the people pay ; that it has throughout our history attempted to solve social problems, and is doing so still ; and that it is as sure as anything human can be that if it did not interfere in certain cases to aid the struggling, to put a curb upon the tyrannous, and to regulate divers specified affairs, the poor and the helpless would be the principal sufferers, and greed of gain and lust of power would be in the ascendant.

But it would be easy to push this interference too far. Admitted that the State has done certain things for us, and, in the main, done them well, this affords no argument that it should do everything in the hope that equal success would follow. There is an assumption dear to pedants and schoolboys that because one does *this* he is bound to do *that*, but neither our daily lives nor our State concerns are or ought to be so governed. They are largely regulated by circumstances, with the idea of doing the best possible under existing conditions. For there is no infallible scheme of government or of society, and the system must be made to suit the people and not the people to suit the system.

And although the State, in certain departments of its interference, has done well, it has not brilliantly succeeded where it has entered into competition with private enterprise. Just as public companies are worked at a greater cost than the same concerns in the hands of individual proprietors, so Government enterprises are always highly expensive and often disastrous failures. It did not need the recent revelations concerning the waste, the jobbery, and the wanton extravagance of certain of our departments to inform those who knew anything of the public offices or the Government dockyards, that such things were the customary results of the system. Stroll through a private dockyard and then through a public one ; visit a large mercantile office and then a Government department in Whitehall ; and decide whether the State is a model master. It may be said that it is simply the system that is to blame, but surely the universality of evil result from the same cause should teach a lesson.

There may be asserted the possible exception of the Post-office to the charge that the State fails where it competes with private enterprise ; and no one would deny that that department does good work, and that, if all others were like it, there would be less reason to complain. But it must not be forgotten that the Post-office, as far as the main portion of its business—letter-carrying—is concerned, does not compete with private enterprise, for it possesses by law the monopoly of the work ; and that the cheapness of postage, upon which it prides itself, is largely secured by making the people of London pay at least twice as much as they would if competition existed for the letters they send among themselves, in order that they and others may, for the same money, forward letters to Perth or Penzance. As to the Government monopoly of the telegraphs, the result, while beneficial in a certain degree, has had this effect—it has partially strangled the telephone system ; and that will hardly be claimed as a triumph.

Any suggestion, therefore, for making the State interfere still further with private enterprise ought to be most carefully weighed. The question really is whether it has not already done as much in this direction as it ought, and whether, generally speaking, the limits now laid down are not sufficiently broad.

What it does is this : it undertakes by means of an army and navy our external defence ; secures by the police our internal safety ; makes provision by which no person need starve ; enforces upon all a certain amount of education ; and enjoins a set of sanitary regulations for the protection of the community from infectious or contagious disease. These are the main items of its work, but beyond them it provides the means of communication by post and telegraph ; fixes in certain degree the fares on railways and the price of gas ; encourages thrift by the institution of savings banks ; and gives us all an opportunity for religious exercise by the provision of an Established Church.

The objectionable part of this is that which directly interferes with personal opinion or private enterprise. The noble saying of Cromwell—" The State, in choosing men to serve it, takes no notice of their opinions ; if they be willing faithfully to serve it, that satisfies "—spoken before its time, as even some of the Protector's friends may have considered, must now be extended to the contention that the State has no concern whatever with the opinions of its citizens, and that it ought not to endow any sect at the expense of the rest. Concerning the competition with private enterprise, the State, in providing a system of national education and a postal and telegraph service, has gone to the verge of what it should do in such a direction.

While, therefore, the State should not abandon any function it now exercises, the severest caution ought to be used before another is undertaken. All attempts of the ruling power to interfere too closely with the private concerns of men—as witness the sumptuary laws and those against usury—have defeated themselves, and it is not for us to revive systems of interference which, even in the Middle Ages, broke down. It is no answer that some things are going so badly that State-interference may be considered absolutely necessary, and that it is merely the extremity of nervousness that hinders the experiment being tried. Caution is not cowardice, and no man is called upon to be foolhardy to prove his freedom from fear.

When it is said that, in certain directions, matters have come to such a pass that the State must more actively interfere, let us note that extremes meet upon this as upon so many other matters ; for the cry that " the country is going to the dogs " is nowadays raised as lustily by some friends of the working man as ever it has been by the retired colonels and superannuated admirals whose exclusive possession it was so long. And the remedy suggested is that the State should do this, that, and the other, with an utter ignoring of the fact, which all history proves, that the creation of an additional army of officials would strangle enterprise and stifle invention. Thus from the general, it will be necessary to go to the particular, and to ask how far the proposed remedy would be effectual. The principle here argued is that the State should concern itself simply with external defence, internal safety, the protection of those unable to guard themselves, and the undertaking of such work for the general good as cannot be better·done by private enterprise; and this principle holds good against many a nostrum now put forward as an infallible remedy for social ills.

# XXXIII.—SHOULD THE STATE REGULATE LABOUR OR WAGES?

AMONG the many social questions which the pressure of circumstances may soon make political is that of the State regulation
of the hours of labour. The president of the Trades Union
Congress for 1887 advocated, for instance, the passing of an
Eight Hours Bill ; and it is desirable to consider whether this
would in any respect be a step in a right direction.

The argument for such a measure appears in principle to be
this : that the classes dependent upon manual labour for their
livelihood have too many hands for the work there is to do ;
that those who do get work toil too long ; and that both evils
would be remedied by restricting the hours of labour, more men
thus finding employment and all working well within their
strength.

Against these points may be set others : that England has
already been severely affected by competition with countries
where the hours are longer and the pay less ; that any further
restriction of hours without a corresponding reduction of pay
would be ruinous to our trade ; and that it is highly probable that the majority of workmen would prefer to labour for
nine hours at their present wages than for eight hours at less
The last contention, of course, might be answered by an enactment fixing not only the hours to be worked but the wages to
be paid. If this is wished for, it should be clearly put ; but
before any step is taken towards either such measure, several
points concerning each, which now appear more than doubtful,
should be made clear.

A fallacy underlying much of the contention in favour of any such enactment is the idea that the community is divided into two distinct classes—the producing and the consuming. As a fact, there are no producers who do not consume, though there are some consumers who do not produce. But is even that an unmixed evil? There is a further fallacy which arbitrarily divides us into capitalists and labourers ; but every man who can purchase the result of another's labour is a capitalist, and that much-denounced person will never be got rid of as long as it is easier to buy than to make.

A third class which secures the condemnation of many is "the middle-man." It is easy to denounce him, but he is a necessity at once of commerce and of comfort. If one wants some coffee at breakfast, he cannot go to Java for the berry, the West Indies for the sugar, the dairy-farm for the milk, and the Potteries for the cup from which to drink. So far from the middle-man unduly increasing the price of those articles, he lessens it by dealing in bulk with what it would pay neither the producer nor the purchaser to deal with in small quantities ; and not only lessens the price but, in regard to the commodities of a distant land, renders it practically possible for us to have them at all.

It is equally useless to rail at competition as if it were inherently evil, for there will be competition as long as men exist to struggle for supremacy. And competition keeps the world alive, as the tide prevents the sea from stagnating. Occasionally the waves break their bounds, and loss and tribulation result ; but the power for good must not be ignored, because the power for evil is sometimes prominent.

To talk of the working classes as if they thought and acted in a body is another delusion. Not only this. The frequent assumption that somebody or other can speak on behalf of "the people" is a mistake. When it is done, one is entitled to ask what the phrase means ? "The people" are the whole body of the population, and no one section, even if a majority has a right to exclusively claim the title. In legislating, regard must be had to the interests of all and not to those of a part, however numerous ; and this brings us straight to the question of interfering by enactment with the price or the amount of labour.

It is curious to note that the demand which is now being raised by some Trade Unionists on behalf of labour is similar in principle to that which was used for centuries by the propertied classes against labour. The Statute of Labourers, passed in the reign of Edward III., fixed wages in most precise fashion, settling that of a master mason, for instance, at fourpence and of journeymen masons at threepence a day. And as lately as only eight years after George III. came to the throne, all master tailors in London and for five miles round were forbidden under heavy penalties from giving, and their workmen from accepting, more than 2s. 7½d. a day—except in the case of a general mourning. Subsequently, statesmen grew more wise, and, in the closing years of last century, the younger Pitt refused to support a bill to regulate the wages of labourers in husbandry. But it is singular that, whereas Adam Smith could say that "whenever the Legislature attempts to regulate the difference between masters and their workmen, its counsellors are always the masters," to-day it is the workmen who promise to become so.

If it be replied that it is State interference with the hours alone and not with the wages that is demanded, it may be submitted that if the one is done it will be a hardship to the worker rather than a boon if the other be not attempted. For, if a man, by working nine hours a day, could earn, say, 27s. a week, it is obvious that for eight hours a day he would not earn more in the same period than 24s., unless Parliament insisted that he should receive the higher sum for the less work. But is Parliament likely to do anything of the kind ; if it did do it, would, it be found to be practicable ; and, if it were found to be practicable, would it be just ?

Parliament is not likely to do anything of the kind, because the experience of centuries has taught us that it is impossible to fix wages by statute. It was tried over and over again, first by enactments applying to the whole country, and then by regulations for each county, settled by the local justices of the peace ; but, though the experiment was backed by all the forces of law, it broke down so utterly that in time it had to be got rid of.

Even if the return could be secured of a majority to Parliament pledged to the proposal, would it be likely to be any
more practicable to-day than it was in olden times ? We
are now an open market for the world. If hours were lessened
and wages not reduced, imported articles from foreign countries
would become much cheaper than our own goods, and would be
bought to the detriment of English workers. Is it proposed
by the promoters of a compulsory eight-hours working day that
we should have Protection once more, and a prohibitory tariff
placed upon all manufactured goods brought from abroad in
order to keep up the price of English articles ?

And, further, if it were practicable, would it be just ? It would
be unjust to the employers, who would have to pay present
prices for lessened work ; it would be unjust to the toilers, in
that it would prevent them from making a higher income by
working more ; and it would be unjust to the consumers, in
making them give a greater price for the commodities they
required. Those who propose the compulsory eight hours
would presumably wish wages to be maintained at the present
standard ; it would hardly be a popular cry if it would have
the effect of bringing wages down.

If the Legislature is to interfere at all in this direction, the old
proposal had better be put forward at once—

> Eight hours' work, eight hours' play,
> Eight hours' sleep, and eight shillings a day.

This, at least, would have the merit of simplicity, and the more
comprehensive proposal is as just and as practicable as the
limited one now put forward. But even as to the limited one,
it would be well to know how far and to what persons it would
be applied. If the answer is " The working classes," the further
question is " How are these to be defined ? " Sailors, for instance, are working men, but no one would seriously propose to
apply the eight hours' system to them. Granting they form an
extreme exception, how are we to deal with shopkeepers and all
whom they employ? The shopkeepers may be put aside as
"capitalists" or "middle men," and, therefore, undeserving of
sympathy or consideration ; but those behind their counters are

distinctly workers. Are they all to be included in the eight hours' proposal ? If so, either one of two things : the shops will be shut sixteen hours out of the twenty-four, or their keepers will have to employ half as many hands again as they now do. " Good for the unemployed" may be replied, but who would have to pay for the additional labour ? The consumers, of course, for no law is going to be passed keeping tea and sugar, hats and coats at their present price ; and it would be those that live by weekly wages who would thereby suffer the most. And if, in order to obviate such consequences, all who work in shops were to be excluded from the benefits of an Eight Hours Act, it would be grossly unjust that tens of thousands of toilers, as much entitled to consideration as those employed in any factory or mill, should be kept at work in order to minister to the convenience of their fellows, set free from a portion of their labour by the action of Parliament.

And this leads to a consideration of the proposal that all shops, with certain limited exceptions, shall be closed at a given hour. For the general reasons applicable to other employments, any such proposition ought to be strongly opposed. It would be a grievous hardship to the smaller tradesmen, with many of whom the best chance of making a living is after the great establishments have closed, and an intolerable nuisance to the working classes who can only shop at what a legislator might consider a late hour. If attempted to be put in operation, it would necessitate the creation of an army of informers and inspectors to see that it was not evaded, and it would create an amount of annoyance to honest and hard-working traders for which no expected benefits from it could compensate. The small tradesman, threatened by the co-operative society on the one side and the "monster emporium " on the other, has enough to do to live, without being harassed by a law which he would be tempted constantly to evade, and which, if not evaded, might prove his ruin.

Much the same argument may be used concerning a point which, if the State interferes with the hours of labour, is certain to be raised, for it would have to be plainly stated whether all men would be forbidden under penalty to work overtime. If any such proposal is to be made, how is it to be carried out? Are we to have an additional body of inspectors, prying into every man's house to see whether extra work was being done; or is the hateful system of " the common informer " to be revived for the special benefit of working men?

The argument is not weakened by the fact that, in various directions, not only has the Legislature passed enactments interfering with the amount and the price of labour, but that some of these continue in active operation. By means of the Factory Acts, for instance, it has directly intervened for the protection of women and children, and in so doing has been acting within that part of its duty which demands that it shall stand between the unprotected and overwhelming power. But there is no strict parallel between the case of the adult males of the working classes and that of those women and children who have to toil. The former have again and again shown their power of preserving their own interests by combination; and the evils of State interference where it can possibly be avoided appear sufficient to induce the belief that it is to combination that the working classes ought still to trust. If they cannot by this means put down overtime—and as yet they have not been able to do so—they cannot expect their countrymen to raise prices and run the risk of commercial ruin by doing for them what they ought to be able to do for themselves.

# XXXIV.—SHOULD THE STATE INTERFERE WITH PROPERTY?

HAVING dealt with the manner in which the State interferes with labour, which to most is their only property, it is necessary to consider how it deals with capital, which is the fruit of labour, and how it thus interferes with some of what are termed " the rights of property."

This has been done in order to avoid greater ills, as in the case of the fixing of fair rents by judicial courts in Ireland and certain districts of the Highlands of Scotland ; in others to prevent endless dispute and loss, as in the disposal, in specified proportions, of the personal property of those who die without a will ; in a further series to prevent a virtual monopoly from becoming tyrannous, as in the compulsion of railway companies to run certain third-class trains, and not to charge beyond a stated fare, or the restriction of the profits of gas companies to 10 per cent. unless a specified reduction in price is made to the consumers ; in others, yet, for the supposed advantage of a class, as in the custom of primogeniture, which gives all real property (that is, land) to the eldest son of a father who dies intestate ; and, in others, for the presumed benefit of the community, at the expense of individual efforts, as in the limitation of the duration of patents for inventions to seven, fourteen, or twenty-one years, and of copyright in books to forty-two years from the date of publication, or for the author's life and seven years after, whichever of these terms may be the longer.

As to the first three points—the fixing of fair rents in Ireland and the Highlands, the due division of the personal property of those who die without a will, and the limitation of the power of virtual monopolies—there is no need at this day to argue, for

all are irrevocable. As to the fourth, there is no practical disagreement among leading politicians on both sides regarding
the desirability of doing away with the custom of primogeniture, as enforced by law. But as to the fifth, it may be submitted that the State goes too far or not far enough.

Our legislators have been exceedingly tender towards every
description of property except that created by certain of the
highest phases of brain-power. If a man invents a machine
which may save millions to the community, he loses all specific
property in his invention after a given period of years ; if he
writes a book which may elevate mankind, his family are similarly condemned after a certain period to forfeit all claim upon
the fruits of his labour. But if, instead of putting his brain to
such uses, he merely makes a machine or lends a book for hire,
there is no law to step in and deprive him of the profits if
either machine or book lasts a century.

Why this difference ? The theory appears to be that the community is entitled to profit after a certain period by the brains
of its members, when used in the creative or inventive direction ; but if the claim be good, has not the State an equal right
to profit after a similar period by the brains of its members
when used in trading ways ? Why should brains exercised in
one direction be handicapped in comparison with those exercised in another ? The answer may be that the inventor or
author employs no capital, that the trader does, and that, therefore, whatever profit the former is allowed to make is a profit
upon nothing, while in the latter case the profit is directly upon
the capital employed, which ought not to be interfered with.

But this is to adopt the fallacy that capital is necessarily the
same thing as money. The capital of an inventor or an author
is his brains, which he expends upon his invention or his book ;
and the community has exactly the same right to deprive the
widow and the orphan of a fortune because it was made by a lucky
speculation, for instance, forty-two years before, as of their property in a book because it was published that length of time
previous. It is true that the State does not fully exercise this
right, and protects the family of the mere money-maker while it
despoils that of the brain-worker ; but the principle is one which
contains larger possibilities than the former have yet realized.

The argument that it is for the benefit of the community that only a certain amount of time should be given to the inventor or the author in which to make a profit is dangerous, because it can so easily be applied to other species of property. Why not to the body of the machine as well as to its principle, why not to the pages of the book as well as to what they contain? And even if it is never pushed so far, there are certain species of property now protected by the law which will not improbably be attacked upon this same ground of "the benefit of the community" before very long; and it is difficult to see how they can be defended as long as the statutes affecting copyright and patents exist.

The most striking of such kinds of property is that in minerals. A man buys an estate for farming, grazing, or, it may be, purposes of pleasure. Some time afterwards minerals are found beneath it, and, though he has neither placed them there nor may assist to get them out, he is privileged to charge "mining royalties" upon every ton that is raised as long as there is any to be obtained. Why should not his power in this direction be limited? He takes everything and gives nothing; the author or inventor gives everything and takes little. It would be as much for "the benefit of the community" to have the former's minerals after a given period, with no reward to himself, as to have the latter's books or machines. Why, then, should bullion be carefully protected and brains despoiled? If it be replied that when a man has bought a plot of ground it is his to the centre of the earth at one side and to the sky on the other, may it not be submitted that the former portion of the right ought to be restricted, while the latter certainly does not exist, for the law steps in at point after point to control his use of the land between the surface and the sky?

The State, therefore, interferes with property, as it is, in a most material degree: instances of such interference have been scattered through these pages, and the tendency of the future is likely to be towards more than less interference. And there is hardly any that can be proposed, even of the extremest kind, for which it would not be possible to find a precedent.

# XXXV.—OUGHT THE STATE TO FIND FOOD AND WORK FOR ALL?

THE State thus interfering with both capital and labour, it is sometimes contended that its duties ought to be so extended as to find food and work for all. There is a captivating sound about the proposition which has commended it to many without a due weighing of the probable results. It is a matter upon which a hasty generalization, though springing from the purest motives, may do vast harm, and is one, therefore, which all ought most carefully to consider before expressing an opinion upon it.

Cardinal Manning, in an article published in the winter of 1887, carried the theory of the public duty of feeding the hungry to its extremest point in these words—" All men are bound by natural obligations, if they can, to feed the hungry. But it may be said that granting the obligation in the giver does not prove a right in the receiver. To which I answer that the obligation to feed the hungry springs from the natural right of every man to life, and to the food necessary for the sustenance of life. So strict is this natural right that it prevails over all positive laws of property. Necessity has no law, and a starving man has a natural right to his neighbour's bread."

With all deference, the last sentence must be stated to be false, both in logic and morals. If it were true, it would justify immediate raids by the starving upon the nearest baker's shop, and one wonders what the Cardinal would say if he happened to be the baker. Granting that every one has a right to live, there is no equivalent right to live at other people's expense.

It is true that, by our Poor Law, a system has been created by which no one need starve, but that does not justify the theft of bread. There is a preliminary question to be put even in the case of the starving, and that is as to why they are in that condition. If it be because they have been idle, or drunken, or generally worthless, as in many cases it is, the mere fact that they are starving does not entitle them to sack a baker's shop. They will be fed by the Poor Law if they take the necessary steps, but if they are able-bodied they will have to work for their food ; and as most human beings have to do the same, where is the hardship ?

It will be replied by some that the Poor Law works harshly towards the deserving poor, but that is an argument for amendment, not for abolition or indiscriminate extension. And if it be further said that the food supplied is meagre and the lodgings rough, it must be remembered that the poor-rate is paid by a very large number whose food is no more plentiful and whose lodgings are certainly worse. As for the argument that some people starve rather than "enter the house," it is not easy to see what relief could be given by the State without infringing that spirit.

But there is a question most intimately affecting this matter which, though of the highest importance, cannot be discussed here as it deserves, and that is the question of population, concerning which Mill truly says, " Every one has a right to live. We will suppose this granted. But no one has a right to bring creatures into life, to be supported by other people. Whoever means to stand upon the first of these rights must renounce all pretension to the last. If a man cannot support even himself unless others help him, those others are entitled to say that they do not also undertake the support of any offspring which it is physically possible for him to summon into the world. . . . It would be possible for the State to guarantee employment at ample wages to all who are born. But if it does this, it is bound in self-protection, and for the sake of every purpose for which government exists, to provide that no person shall be born without its consent. . . . It cannot, with impunity, take the feeding upon itself and leave the multiplying free."

And so, while the Poor Law ought to be carried out in the humanest and most liberal fashion compatible with the interests of the poor who pay the rates as well as the poor who benefit by them, any movement for so extending it as to bring more persons under its operation, and thus to further pauperize the community, would be dangerous. We had enough of that under the system swept away by the Act of 1834, the hideous demoralization caused by which should be studied to-day by those who are eager for a freer dispensation of State relief.

The arguments against the State going further than at present in the direction of giving food to all are equally good as against providing work for all. Relief works have ever been centres of corruption and waste of the worst type, while "national workshops" have not been so brilliant a success in the form of dock-yards and arsenals as to warrant an extension of the system to all the trades we practise.

The theory that the State is bound to provide work for all was never more concisely put than in the original draft of the French Republican Constitution after the Revolution of 1848, the seventh article of which ran thus : " The right of labour is the right which every man has to live by his labour. It is the duty of Society, through the channels of production and other means at its command, hereafter to be organized, to provide work for such able-bodied men as cannot find it for themselves." But even a Government imbued with Socialistic tendencies found this to be much too strong, and modified it thus : "It is the duty of Society by fraternal assistance to protect the lives of necessitous citizens, either by finding them work as far as possible, or by providing for those who are incapacitated for work and who have no families to support them." Yet the modified form was not found to work well in actual practice, and the history of the failure of the French National Workshops of 1848 remains as an eloquent testimony to the fact that the State ought to interfere as little as possible with industrial enterprises and private concerns.

# XXXVI.—HOW OUGHT WE TO DEAL WITH SOCIALISM?

EVEN the considerations already put forward do not exhaust the social question, for only in the briefest fashion have been touched the important points which that question involves. And there is yet left to be discussed the attitude which ought to be adopted towards that body of opinions upon public affairs vaguely known as "Socialism."

The attitude of some is simply denunciatory, for there is a class of politician which always imputes base motives to those with whom it disagrees, and which is so proficient in abuse that it apparently thinks it a waste of time to argue. That class has been painfully in evidence in regard to the Socialists. It is considered that—so true is the old proverb that if you give a dog a bad name you may as well hang him—nothing more need be done respecting a new and therefore unpopular doctrine than to so label it as to ensure its repudiation by honest but unthinking men. And thus the name "Socialist" is applied as equivalent to thief ; and men utterly ignorant of what the words imply link Socialist to Nihilist, Communist to Anarchist, as if each were equal to each, and all therefore equal to one another.

This has been the favourite device of the opponents of all new doctrines, political or social, philosophical or religious. To be ridiculed, to be persecuted, even to be slain has been the fate of the would-be elevators of their kind, as the roll of fame, which includes the names of Socrates and Galileo, Luther and Savonarola, Voltaire and Roger Bacon, Mazzini and Darwin will testify. The Socialists now are hardly called worse names than were applied to geologists fifty years ago, and to

Evolutionists but the other day. Atheists, of course, they have been named, for Atheist is the epithet customarily applied by ignorant and bigoted men, who have made God in their own image, to those more zealous in endeavouring to raise humanity.

Against any such method of dealing with public questions all fair-minded men should strongly, and without ceasing, protest. And as Socialism is spreading among the masses, it is in the highest degree important that the fact should be studied calmly and without prejudice. Hard words break no bones, and con-tumely tends to strengthen any cause in which there is an atom of good.

Socialism, therefore, should be dealt with in an inquiring and not an abusive spirit, and with the determination to accept from it whatever of good to the community we may find it to contain. There is another method which Prince Bismarck has been trying for years, and with the signal lack of success that always comes from trying to stamp out an opinion by force of law. In presumed defence of "society" and "order"—two excellent things, but often the excuse for despots to perpetrate cruel injustice upon the liberty-loving and the poor—he has secured law after law for the purpose of "putting down Socialism;" men have been torn from their homes because of their opinions; the right of public meeting has been placed at the mercy of the police; the press has been gagged, and every means taken to stamp out a body of opinions some of which even the German Chancellor himself cannot help sharing. And with what result? That, after ten years of this wretched work, the Socialists—though prevented from public meeting, speaking, or writing—are multiplying in Germany in an ever-growing proportion; that in Berlin, the capital of the empire, they number tens of thousands of electors as their adherents; and that Prince Bismarck is ever asking for extended powers to crush a force which, in its free state, as yielding to the touch as water, is mighty when compressed.

With an even greater power of police, and no restriction at all from the laws, the Czar has failed as signally to extirpate Nihilism. Ideas cannot be killed in this fashion, though their holders can be and are rendered more dangerous. Mill certainly considered that "the dictum that truth always triumphs over persecution is one of those pleasant falsehoods which men repeat after one another till they pass into commonplaces, but which all experience refutes;" and he was of opinion that "no reasonable person can doubt that Christianity might have been extirpated in the Roman Empire." But it may be submitted that, when arguing about the persecution of ideas to-day, we must not forget the immense additional force given to them by means of printing. The secret presses of Germany and Russia "spread the light;" and there is nothing so certain as that the very charm which comes from the possession of that which is prohibited aids in strengthening a movement which is under the ban of the law.

But, it may be said, the efforts of those who would attempt to put down Socialism are not to be considered in the light of political persecution, and are not to be compared with religious persecution, for they are directed solely to the suppression of "anti-social" doctrines, the adoption of which would be fatal not only to States as they now exist, but to society itself. A more precise definition must be asked, however, of the doctrines thus described. Though opposed to an eight hours' bill, to land nationalization, and to national workshops, leading points in the Socialist programme, I cannot conceive how, if they were all adopted within the next year, such dire results could from them flow.

Every new body of doctrine which gives hope to the masses and threatens the domination of the privileged among men has been described with equal virulence by its antagonists. Read the charges upon which Christians were condemned under the Roman Empire; read those brought against Luther and his co-reformers when first Protestantism threatened the Church of Rome; remember those thrown at the Puritans when they tried to secure for Englishmen liberty of thought and action. They were in every case that the doctrines were anti-social; that if adopted they would wreck the then condition of society; and that they were in the highest degree perilous to the State. For it is the fate of all preachers of a new doctrine to be treated as rogues until their persecutors are proved to be fools.

Admittedly there are some theories advanced by men calling themselves Socialists which, if adopted, would seriously conflict with the existing order of society ; but to condemn every proposal put forward as Socialist because there are Socialists who have said strange, and sometimes stupid, things would be monstrous. It is a controversial trick of a peculiarly poor order to attempt to hold the leaders of any movement responsible for the hare-brained ideas of some of their followers. Not to repudiate them is not to signify agreement, or our party leaders would possess some of the most extravagant doctrines ever conceived by man.

Besides, one must always sever the conventional beliefs from the real. No sensible person considers Christianity untrue because even the churches would regard him as a madman who literally adopted the injunction to sell all that he had to give to the poor. In any body of doctrines there are always some which its adherents hold, but do not stand by.

And, therefore, charity as well as common sense demands that the tall talk on both sides—for there is not a great deal to choose between them in this respect—should cease ; but the trick is too easily learned to be quickly dropped. The idea of the well-to-do that all would go smoothly if it were not for " agitators " and " mob-orators " is as absurd as the contention of the Socialist that most of our ills are due to the " profit-monger." Your " agitator " or your " mob-orator " would have not the least influence if he did not voice the feelings, the longings, and the hopes of his silent friends. And as for the " profit-monger," is not the workman who is better off than the poorest among his fellows deserving the name ?

Let us have fair play all round to ideas as well as to men. If, in the supposed interests of society, every movement designed to upraise the poor is suppressed. the tendency must be to force men towards Anarchism and Nihilism, by causing them to wish to destroy that order of things which to them acts so unjustly. Despair is a fatal counsellor, and those who would identify the welfare of the State with that of the mere money-getter are its frequent cause. It is easier to raise the devil than to lay him, and appeals to the merely animal instinct in man—whether to protect his own property or to take that of others, with a complete ignoring of his duties as well as his rights—must end in ruin and shame.

" There is among the English working classes," once observed Sir Robert Peel, " too much suffering and too much perplexity. It is a disgrace and a danger to our civilization. It is absolutely necessary that we should render the condition of the manual labourer less hard and less precarious. We cannot do everything, but something may be effected, and something ought to be done." Though nearly forty years have passed since that statesman's death, we are still groping blindly for the something which ought to be done for the poor ; and such strength as Socialism possesses is derived from the general spread of the feeling which Peel put into words, and which no politician—much more no statesman—can afford to neglect.

And that is why the politics of the future will be largely affected by the social questions now coming to the front. From the opinions of many who are pressing them forward one may profoundly differ, but justice demands that all they advance should be examined without prejudice, and with the determination to accept that which is good, from whatever quarter it may come.

# XXXVII.—WHAT SHOULD BE THE LIBERAL PROGRAMME?

WHILE the social problem, however, is developing, we have the political problem to face ; and, therefore, the immediate programme of the Liberal party now demands consideration. In some detail have been presented the arguments from a Liberal point upon all the great public questions which are either ripe or ripening for settlement. It has not been possible to go minutely into every point involved ; a broad outline of each subject has had to suffice ; but it may be trusted that each has been sufficiently explained for us now to consider which should occupy the forefront in the Liberal platform.

Mr. Bright observed, in days not long since, when he was honoured by every man in the party as one of its most trusted leaders, that he disliked programmes. What he preferred, it was evident, was that when some great question—such as the repeal of the Corn Laws or the extension of the suffrage, with both of which his name will be ever identified—should thrust itself to the front by force of circumstances, it should be faced by the Liberal party and dealt with on its merits ; and what he opposed, it was equally evident, was the formulation of any cut-and-dried programme, containing a number of points to be accepted as a shibboleth by every man calling himself Liberal or Radical, and by its hide-bound propensity tending to retard real progress.

The Irish question is one of those great matters which has thrust itself to the front by force of circumstances, which should be faced by the Liberal party and dealt with on its merits, and which, until it is so faced and dealt with, will stand in the path of any real reforms. The evil effects of the discontent of four millions of people at our very doors are not to be got rid of by shutting our eyes to them ; and the intensification of those evil effects which is to-day going on is a matter which must engage the attention of every Liberal.

But, out of dislike for any cut-and-dried programme of several measures to be accepted wholesale and without question, the party must not be allowed to drift into aimlessness. As long as it exists it must exist for work, and its fruit must not be phrases but facts. Liberalism can never return to the days when it munched the dry remainder biscuit of worn-out Whiggery. A hide-bound programme may be a bad thing, but nothing worse can be imagined than the string of airy nothings which used to do duty for a policy among the latter-day Whigs. Take the addresses issued by them at the general election of 1852 as an instance, and which have been effectively summarized thus :—" They promised (in the words of Sir James Graham) ' cautious but progressive reform,' and (in those of Sir Charles Wood) ' well-advised but certain progress.' Lord Palmerston said he trusted the new Liberal Government would answer ' the just expectation of the country,' and Lord John Russell pledged it to ' rational and enlightened progress.' "

Now, in these days, we want something decidedly more definite than that, and, if our leaders could offer us nothing better, we should have either to find other leaders or abandon our aims. Happily we need do neither, for the Liberal chiefs, with Mr. Gladstone at their head, are prepared to advance with the needs of the times, and to advocate those measures which the circumstances demand and their principles justify.

In the forefront of our efforts at this moment stands, and must continue to stand until it is settled, the question of self-government for Ireland. Stripped of all quarrel upon point of detail, the Liberal party is pledged, while upholding the unity of the Empire and the supremacy of the Imperial Parliament, to give the sister country a representative body sitting in Dublin to deal with exclusively Irish affairs. The day cannot be long delayed when an attempt must be made to place the local government of Ireland upon a sounder and broader basis than at present. When it arrives, the Liberal party has its idea ready. Details can be compromised ; the principle cannot be touched. For Liberals are convinced that, by whatever name it may be called, and by whatever party it may be introduced, Home Rule must come, and that, for the sake of all the interests involved, Imperial and Irish, it will be in the highest degree desirable to grant it frankly and fully, with due regard to the interests concerned.

Linked with this point is another regarding Ireland upon which the Liberal party will entertain not the smallest doubt. The Coercion Act has been used for partisan purposes by dependent and often incompetent magistrates, and it must be repealed. Upon this point there can be no compromise. Every man hoping to be returned by Liberal votes at the next election must pledge himself to the immediate, total, and unconditional repeal of the Crimes Act of 1887.

The next item in the accepted Liberal programme is the disestablishment of the Church in Wales, as well as of the Scottish Kirk. Each is a purely domestic matter which ought to be settled according to the wishes of the majority of the people affected. As to the wishes of Wales, no one can have a doubt ; and though the declaration of Scotland, through its representatives, is not so emphatic, it is sufficiently clear for Liberals to support the demand.

But, after all, these points touch only Ireland, Wales, and Scotland. England is the largest portion of this kingdom, and its claims must not be ignored. A great Parisian editor used to say that the description of a woman run over on the Boulevards was of more interest to his readers than that of a battle on the Nile. It would be well if politicians would take this idea to heart. Little use is it to talk of the despotism practised in Ireland, of the hardships endured by the crofters in Scotland, and of the injustice done to the tithepayers in Wales, if we are not prepared to apply the same principles to London as to Limerick, to Chester as to Cardigan, and to Liverpool as to the Lews. The average man will not be satisfied of the sincerity of those who keep their eyes fixed upon distant places, and are full of sympathy for the oppressed who are afar off, but can spare no time for the grievances existing at their doors.

And as, therefore, if Liberalism is to be again in the ascendant in the councils of the Empire, England must be won, it is well to emphasize the contention that England will never be won by a party which ignores her wants. Home Rule for Ireland, disestablishment for Scotland and Wales, are good things, and they will have to be granted when our majority comes ; but what will that majority do for England ?

Without attempting to lay down a programme, it may be said that there is one English problem to which Liberalism will have at once to apply itself, and that is the problem of the land. The time is past for talking comfortable platitudes upon this matter, for we find that Tories can do that as glibly as Liberals, and with the same lack of good result. The very least that can be demanded—in addition to the abolition of the custom of primogeniture and an extensive simplification of the process of transfer—is a thorough reform of the laws affecting settlement, the taxing of land at death in the same proportion as other descriptions of property, the placing of the land tax upon a basis more remunerative to the Exchequer, and a large measure of leasehold enfranchisement. And when candidates talk in future of being in favour of "land reform," they must be definitely pinned down as to their views upon such points as these.

That Free Trade will remain a plank in the Liberal platform, not to be dropped or tampered with, goes without saying. It is a point as much beyond question as the existence of Parliament itself, and concerning it as much cannot be observed as regarding the latter. For, while our trade system must remain free, both Houses stand in need of reform. The Lords, in Mr. John Morley's phrase, must be mended or ended, and the path of legislative progress in the Commons made more smooth. The laws in every way affecting the return of members to the latter likewise stand sorely in need of reform, and that reform cannot be ignored by the Liberal party.

Further, Liberals are agreed that localities shall have greater power in various directions, and upon the liquor traffic in especial, of deciding upon their own affairs. The tendency of recent days has been to take these out of the hands of those most intimately concerned, and to vest supreme power in a body of Government clerks at Whitehall. That is a tendency which must be reversed. We are advocating decentralization in regard to Ireland ; we are being led to advocate it in regard to Wales and Scotland ; England must similarly be benefited, and the red-tape of Whitehall unwound from our purely local concerns.

Peace and Retrenchment must continue to be inscribed on the Liberal banner as well as Reform. Preference for international arbitration over war must distinguish our party ; a determination to be as free as possible from all entangling engagements with foreign powers must always be with us. And there must ever be displayed a resolve to place the Government service upon the same business-like and efficient basis as private concerns, to get rid of the notion that it is work to be lightly undertaken and highly paid, and to emphasize the contention that the taxbearer shall have full value from every one of his servants for the wages he pays.

Above all, the greatest care must be taken by every Liberal to preserve—aye, and to extend—individual liberty. Men cannot dance in fetters, and all enactments which unnecessarily hinder the development of private enterprise, and all traditions which interfere with the fullest enjoyment of the rights of speech and action, must be swept away.

While thus giving our attention to the more purely political questions as they arise, Liberals must never forget that the poor we always have with us. Ours is a gospel of hope for the oppressed ; it must equally be a gospel of hope for the hard-working. We want our working men to be civil, not servile ; our working women to use courtesy, and not a curtsey. We wish to see the end of a system by which a bow is rewarded with a blanket and a curtsey with coal. The man who too frequently bends his back is likely to become permanently affected with a stoop, and the old order of hat-touching, bowing, and scraping must disappear. We do not deny that it is right that men should respect others, but it is often forgotten that it is equally right that they should respect themselves.

14

In dealing with things social, as well as things political, we must always remember that it is flesh and blood with which in the result we have to deal. Some thinkers ignore sentiment, do not believe in kindness, and treat men like machines, forgetting that even machines require oil. It is not for philosophers with homes and armchairs and a settled income to ask whether life is worth living ; that question is for the poor and the lowly and the down-trodden, to whom the struggle for existence is not a matter for theorizing or moral-drawing, but is a never-ending, heart-breaking, soul-destroying reality.

So, if Liberalism is to live, it must be liberal in fact as well as in name. A Liberal who talks of equal rights on the platform and swears at his servants at home, who waxes wroth against a national oppressor and treats those poorer than himself like serfs, is as little deserving of respect as a Liberal policy which solely considers the externals of either liberty or life. A programme based upon such a policy must fail, and deserves to fail ; and if we are to have a platform at all, it must be one upon which the rich man and the son of toil can stand side by side.

## XXXVIII. — HOW IS THE LIBERAL PROGRAMME TO BE ATTAINED?

It is natural to ask how, when the Liberal programme has been framed, it is to be attained. Measures no more come with wishing than winds with whistling ; and if our principles are to be put into practice, it will only be by our joining those of similar mind.

Not every politician, even if his ideas be sound, is a practical man. The disposition to insist that no bread is better than half a loaf is one that commends itself to me neither in business nor in daily life, but it is one upon which many a man of Liberal leanings acts, to the detriment of the principles he professes to hold dear. Insistence upon the one point to the exclusion of the ninety-nine, and readiness to join enemies who disagree on the whole hundred rather than friends who disagree on only the one, are qualities unpleasantly prominent in many otherwise worthy men. It cannot too often be urged that politics, like business or married life, can only be carried on by occasional give-and-take. The partner who persists in always having his own way ; the husband who is ever asserting authority over his wife ; and the politician who will never yield an iota to his friends—all are alike objectionable, and deserve no particle of consideration from those around them.

A spurious independence is another hindrance in the path of progress. Faith without works is occasionally worth commendation in public life ; but one must be certain that the faith is genuine, and for most political "independence," that cannot be claimed. Diseased vanity, disappointed ambition, and deliberate place-hunting have more to do with that kind of thing than devotion to principle. "The fact is that individualism is very often a mere cloak for selfishness ; it is the name with which pedants justify the pragmatic intolerance which will not yield one jot of personal claim or unsatisfied vanity to secure the triumph of the noblest cause and the highest principles." When Mr. Chamberlain wrote those words he was undoubtedly right.

Whenever, therefore, one is called upon to admire some outburst of independence which splits a political party or hinders the progress of a cause, he should look very closely at the history of those concerned. He should not forget that, just as there are people who are much too independent to touch their hats for civility, though they would for a sixpence, there are politicians who are far too spirited to stick to their party but not to bid for place. Happily these latter seem never able to avoid using certain stock phrases, which should put others on their guard. When a man says he prefers country to party, or vaunts that his motto is "measures not men," he lays himself open to just suspicion, because he talks as political impostors have long been accustomed to talk ; when he proclaims his readiness to recognize the virtues of his enemies, you may be certain that he will speedily show himself keenly alive to the failings of his friends ; and a politician never begins to boast that he is a representative and not a delegate until he has ceased to represent the opinions of those who sent him to Parliament.

More estimable than these, but still people who must not be allowed to hamper the operations of the Liberal party, are the constitutional pedant and the rigid doctrinaire. Nothing is more lamentable than the endeavours of the former to prove by precedent that nothing ought to be done in the nineteenth century differently to how it was done in the seventeenth ; and nothing more filled with the promise of disappointment than the theorizings of the latter as to what measures would secure us a perfect State.

It is with persons as well as with principles that we have to deal, and in politics we must not despise the humblest instruments. History, like the coral reef, is made grain by grain and day by day, and often by agents as comparatively insignificant. The old idea that the people's leaders must come from "the governing classes," or, better still, "the governing families," does not harmonize with democratic institutions. As to "the governing families" part of it, that may be brushed aside at once as being as absurd in theory as it is untrue to all recent English history; for who have been our most brilliant and successful statesmen since the present fashion of constitutional government was established? Who were Walpole, Pitt, Burke, Fox, Canning, Peel, Cobden, Gladstone, and Disraeli? Even as this book is written the Tories in the House of Commons are nominally led by Mr. Smith, and practically by Mr. Goschen. The instinct of the people has taught them the best leaders, as it has taught them the best principles.

A clear-headed working man is a better political counsellor than a muddle-minded peer. There are plenty of working men who are not clear-headed, as there are plenty of peers who are not muddled of mind; but the instinct of the mass is far more likely to be sound than that of the class. In the course of English history the masses have usually been right and the classes wrong. The former have been less selfish, more ready to redress injuries, and keener to oppose tyranny. And even where the masses have been in the wrong, it has often been because their instinctive sense of right has led them to sympathize with a man or a cause, undeserving of regard, but apparently exposed to the persecutions of the great.

Thus, in order to make the Liberal cause succeed, zeal must be combined with unity and toleration with courage, and our energies must be so concentrated by organization as to make them most effective when battle is joined. For the private soldiers in the great army of progress, there is no advice so sedulously to be rejected as that of Talleyrand, "Above all, no zeal." If there is not within Liberals a burning desire to forward their principles, they have no right to complain if those principles stand still. A Liberal who is lukewarm is like a joint half-cooked—of no practical service until possessed of more heat; and it is the duty of every earnest man among us to keep the political oven at baking point.

But with zeal there must be unity. Differences on details must not be allowed to separate friends. There is not always a sufficiency of tolerance displayed towards those who do not see eye to eye with the others. Agreement in principle is the pass-key which should open to all Liberals the door to unity with their brethren ; divergence on detail should be settled inside. "Take heed," said Cromwell, " of being sharp, or too easily sharpened by others, against those to whom you can object little but that they square not with you in every opinion concerning matters of religion." To no modern Liberal can his principles be dearer than was his religion to Cromwell, and the great champion of liberty's words ought to be laid to heart by each one of us.

With all toleration, there must be no lack of courage. It is not asked of most to make sacrifices in the Liberal cause, far less to become martyrs in its behalf ; but unless the martyr-spirit remains to the party, ready for action should occasion arise, Liberalism will wither into wastedness. But even courage will fail of its result without concentration, for the undisciplined mass is no match for the disciplined army. To succeed, there must be organization ; and if Liberals will not associate for common purposes they will deserve to be beaten. All holders of progressive principles ought to attach themselves to the Liberal Association of their own constituency ; if there is a Radical Club as well, they cannot do better than join it ; for the more links that exist between all sections of the party, the stronger will be the bond uniting them. Personal likes or dislikes ought not to affect men in the matter. A Liberal is not worthy the name who, because he is not asked to the house of the president of the local association, declines to join ; and equally unworthy of it is he who, because he does not ask the president of the Radical Club to his own house, objects to put up for memberhip. Personal and social considerations of this kind are out of place in politics, and a man's freedom from them may almost be taken as a test of the reality of his Liberalism.

There are many ready to criticize those who do a party's work, but who never lift a finger to assist their efforts. These are the beings who, at election times, hinder the helpers by carpings, who are never slow to assume a share of credit in case of victory, and are ever eager to throw the blame upon others in event of defeat. Battles are not won by such as these. Every Liberal to whom his principles are dear should show it by joining with his fellows, striving his hardest in his own constituency, and never ceasing to display in his life and by his works that Liberalism to him is not a name but a principle, increasingly dear as it is hampered by desertion, threatened with danger, or in peril of defeat. If he did that, there would be needed no further answer to the question, " How is the Liberal Programme to be attained ? " for what was required would have been accomplished.

# XXXIX. — IS PERFECTION IN POLITICS POSSIBLE?

It is sometimes asked whether, after all the struggling of public life, perfection in politics is possible. But in what department of human affairs *is* perfection possible? Is it in medicine? Mark the proportion of those born who die before they are five years old. Is it in science? The scientist is still engaged, as Newton was, in picking up shells on the shore of a vast ocean of knowledge which he is unable yet to navigate. Is it in religion? Ask the Christian and the Confucian, the Mahommedan and the Buddhist to define the word, before giving an answer. When medicine, and science, and religion have reached universally acknowledged perfection, politics may be hoped to follow in their wake; but until that period it is needless to expect it.

The very idea that it is possible has been the cause of many delusions, and delusions are dangerous. Read Plato's "Republic," More's "Utopia," and Harington's "Oceana," and you will perceive how far the ideal is removed from any conceivable real. It may be that from these works good has flowed, since the evident impossibility of making the whole plan of use has not prevented political thinkers taking from them such ideas as were practicable, and grafting these upon existing institutions, with benefit to the State. But the dreamy schemes of the eighteenth century, the influence of which has not yet died away, were of a different order. For, in the endeavour to change society at a stroke, blunders were made which have caused lasting injury; and these should teach us that the true ideal in politics is that which does not attempt to bend men, or break them if necessary, to suit the machine, but makes the machine to fit the men. The philosopher is a useful personage, but the attempt to rule men from a library customarily results in disaster. The problem of life cannot be solved like a proposition in Euclid ; there, squares always are squares and circles never anything else ; but in every-day existence the square is often forced to be circular by the rubbing off of the angles. And too often it will be found that the philosopher, because of his lack of practical acquaint-ance with his fellow men, exaggerates both what he knows and what he does : he blows a bubble and calls it the globe ; light-ing a candle, he thinks it the sun.

All history teaches that the road to heaven does not lie through Acts of Parliament, and that under the best laws the saints would not be many and the sinners would be far from few. No more pernicious nonsense is talked than that all our social misery, crime, and degradation is due to bad laws. The poli-tical student cannot doubt that much misery may be mitigated, crime prevented, and degradation made impossible by good laws, and it is that knowledge which should stimulate every Liberal to lose no opportunity of improving the conditions under which we live. But it is to display an ignorance of human nature that is really lamentable, or a desire to flatter human weakness that is beneath contempt, to tell the people that, if only certain changes were made in the constitution of the State or of society, all would be well, none would suffer, and crime and poverty would be known only as traditions of the past.

It is not necessary to assert the old theological dogma that, left to himself, man is irredeemably bad, in order to believe that a great many bearing the name are very far from good. There is, unhappily, hardly a family in the country that has not one black sheep—or, at the best, one speckled specimen—to deplore. Do we not all know the idle worthless son of good and hard-working parents, a curse to his own and to all with whom he comes in contact? The laws affecting him are the same as those which affect his brothers : they prosper, he fails.

Why? Because they are worthy, he is worthless ; and there is no conceivable state of society in which he could be, or ought to be, served as well as they. Certainly there are bad men who flourish, and good who wither away; but the political system which should prevent the possibility of this has not yet been invented—and never will be.

Therefore it is one of the most dangerous of political delusions to believe that any possible reform can make all men prosperous and contented. It is just as likely as that this would be brought about by the universal practice of the old distich—

> Early to bed and early to rise
> Makes a man healthy, wealthy, and wise,

as if chimney sweeps, milkmen, and market gardeners had a monopoly of those excellent qualities. The possession of an ideal is a good thing, as long as it is not allowed to overshadow the real ; and those whose ideal causes them to ignore the indolence and vice of their fellows are blind guides who would lead us into a ditch.

Therefore, while perfection in politics will never be realized, and the belief that it can be is fraught with danger, it should be urged upon all to think out the possibilities of the future, and to have a political ideal at which to aim. Mine is a State in which all men shall be equal before the law, every one have a fair chance according to his virtues, his talents, and his industry, and none be advanced because of hereditary or legalized privilege. A State in which all men are free, and wherein there is a fair field and no favour, is that for which Liberals should strive. Even when it is secured we shall still have with us the idle and the vicious, for those specimens of humanity will never perish from out the land ; but the workful and the sober-minded will have a better chance of success than they have to-day, and the State will be benefited thereby.

Extension of individual liberty, abolition of inherited or other privilege—those points really sum up the Liberal ideal. If it be said that it does not promise to fill the people's stomachs, it must be replied that stomach-filling is not the special concern of political life. That is a matter for the people to accomplish ; let us remove every legalized hindrance to their doing it by their own capacities, but when we have done that they must do the stomach-filling for themselves. The State may and does feed the unfortunate, but, if it is to feed the idle, it will have to make the idle work for their food. There is no necessity either in law or in morals to tax those who work for the advantage of those who do not ; and the most perfect State will be that in which the lazy and worthless will be made to labour, and the toilers be protected from being by them despoiled.

What we ask is equality of opportunity, and we have much to do before that can be obtained. There are some who say that they do not believe in elevating the working classes, because it would leave the ground floor of the social edifice untenanted. But the tenants are tired of being on the ground, and wish to see how the upper story justifies its existence, and in that they are right. With equality of opportunity, many to whom we are now called upon by convention to bow will sink to their proper level, while the men who work by brain or hands will acquire their rightful position in the social state. But without the fullest political liberty, this will never be attained, and we must strive jointly for both.

The political ideal at which we should aim is embraced in the words of Lincoln—" that government of the people, by the people, for the people, shall not perish from the earth," and to that may be added that equality of opportunity shall be conceded to each one of us. Let us gain this, and as perfect a State as imperfect human nature can design or deserve will be ours.

# XL.—WHERE SHALL WE STOP?

WHEN the late Lord Shaftesbury was in the House of Commons, and was engaged in the apparently endless task of attempting to reform the factory laws, he brought in a bill to regulate the labour of children in calico-print works. He had already done much, but he wished to do more, and on being asked by his opponents, "Where will you stop?" he replied, "Nowhere, so long as any portion of this gigantic evil remains to be remedied."

In the same spirit may be answered the question sometimes asked as to where Liberals will be prepared to stay the reforming hand. A period cannot be put to progress any more than a limit to literature, or to science a stopping-place. True, we have got rid of the greater tyrannies : divine right of kings, personal rule, borough-mongering—all are dead. We have got rid of the greater inequalities : purchase in the army, nomination in the civil service, have gone the way of the separate form at school, the distinctive tuft at the University, for the sons of peers. We have got rid of the old Tory idea that the people have nothing to do with the laws except to obey them ; we now possess household, we may soon possess adult, suffrage. But are we, therefore, to do no more ? Because we travel faster than our fathers, do we frown upon all improvements in locomotion? Because we no longer suffer from the Plague, the Sweating Sickness, and the Black Death, do the doctors sit with folded arms? No ; for the motto of the race is progress, and until every tyranny, every iniquity, and every inequality which trouble us in public life are vanquished, we cannot in our conscience cease from attack.

Remember always the saying of Turgot, the great French economist, " It is not error which opposes the progress of truth : it is indolence, obstinacy, the spirit of routine, everything that favours inaction." Much that hinders our advance comes from forgetfulness of what Liberalism has done, and what, therefore, it is still capable of doing. A politician once remarked, " Suppose that for but a month after the passing of any great measure of reform, such as the repeal of the Corn Laws, the extension of the suffrage, or the establishment of a national system of education, only the Liberals could have gained the benefit and the Tories been left outside, wouldn't the Tories have joined us in a hurry to help reap the advantage the Liberals had secured ? " There is no doubt as to the answer ; but even as the sun shines upon the unjust as well as upon the just, so the beneficent stream of Liberal legislation fertilizes the waste lands of Toryism equally with the possessions of those who have prepared its course.

Yet it is this forgetfulness against which we have mainly to contend. The age in which we live is so distinguished for progressive sentiment, so noteworthy for the number and the magnitude of its reforms, that even Liberals are occasionally in danger of letting slip some of the good effects which struggle has won by nodding contentedly at the strides that have been taken, heedless of the enemy ever anxious to push back the shadow on the dial. Fortunately for the preservation of our liberties, the drowsiness is seldom allowed to glide into sleep, for an awakening is furnished by the premature shouts of triumph of those whose highest interest would be to remain silent, for it is only thus that success to them is possible.

But while in the calm of supposed security, while, for instance, enjoying the belief that the Crown, as a governing power, is now in England non-existent, we are suddenly aroused by the argument that the possible feelings of the Sovereign with regard to a probable Irish Ministry are to be considered in antagonism to Home Rule ; while we are indulging the hope that Free Trade rests upon as firm a basis as parliamentary government, we see the Conservative party coquetting with Protection ; while we regard equality before the law as practically admitted by all, we have constantly brought to our notice the belief of the county magistrate that that which done by his son would be food for laughter, done by his hind deserves hard labour ; while sunning ourselves with the thought that religious liberty has been absolutely secured, we have witnessed a member of Parliament, thrice elected by a free constituency, thrice rejected by the House of Commons, and even thrown by the police from its doors, upon theological grounds and theological grounds alone ; and while imagining that freedom of speech, of action, and of the press was beyond challenge even by the Tories. men in London have been wounded and imprisoned for asserting the right of public meeting, and many sent to gaol in Ireland for doing that which in England, Wales, and Scotland would be as perfectly legal as it was perfectly right : when we see such things we are brought to recognize that our liberties, after all, hang by a thread.

It is well, however, that we should have these rude awakenings in order to teach us that Toryism is not dead, that it is as ready as ever to seize every opportunity for depriving the people of their liberty, to rivet the yoke of ascendency upon their shoulders, and to subvert that freedom which only slowly and by prolonged struggle has been wrested from the great. The adherents of proscription and privilege do not in these days talk of the divine right of kings—though even that doctrine peeps out when they have occasion to flatter a monarch or an heir-apparent ; but the equally false doctrine of the divine right of Parliaments is persistently put forward, and with the audacious pretence that to dispute it is treason to the democracy. We are told that a House of Commons once chosen can do as it likes for seven years, and no one dare say it "nay ;" that its majority may break the pledges upon which it was elected, may practise coercion where it promised conciliation, may deprive us of every single liberty it was returned to support and extend, and that it is the duty of every good subject to sit with folded arms, to quietly submit to be despoiled of his rights, and to wait with patience until such time as the Prime Minister is

www.ingramcontent.com/pod-product-compliance
Lightning Source LLC
Chambersburg PA
CBHW030327270326
41926CB00010B/1532